Blenheim MK.IF Combat Log

Fighter Command Day Fighter Sweeps/Night Interceptions

September 1939 - June 1940

Hugh Harkins

Blenheim MK.IF
Combat Log

Published by Centurion Publishing
United Kingdom

ISBN 10: 1-903630-56-8
ISBN 13: 978-1-903630-56-3

This volume first published in 2014

The Publisher and Author would like to thank all organisations and services for their assistance and contributions in the preparation of this volume

CONTENTS

INTRODUCTION

The purpose of this volume is to provide a comprehensive detailed study of the operational and combat operations of the RAF's Bristol Blenheim MK.IF twin-engine long-range fighter aircraft from the start of World War II in September 1939 through the battles of May and June 1940 following the German invasion of France and the Low Countries. The volume covers Fighter Commands day fighter sweeps and day/night fighter operations against enemy bombers on both sides of the English Channel, including operations over Dunkirk in the latter part of May and early June covering the evacuation of the British Expeditionary Force. Although primarily aimed at covering Fighter Command Blenheim MK.IF operations, some Coastal Command Blenheim MK.IF and Blenheim MK.IVF combats with enemy aircraft are also detailed when appropriate.

A brief description of the genesis and development of the Bristol Blenheim is laid down, but the volume is not designed to be a comprehensive monograph on that subject. The volume is copiously supported by a wealth of operational documents including Squadron Narratives, Group Intelligence Combat Reports, Squadron operational Records and pilot Personal Combat Reports, many of which are reproduced verbatim. Operational documents have been tied up against German reports whenever possible.

BRISTOL BLENHEIM MK.I

The Bristol Blenheim MK.IF long-range twin-engine fighter was basically a Blenheim MK.I light bomber configured for the fighter role; the Blenheim itself being a development of the Bristol Type 135/142 high-speed twin-engine monoplane designed in 1933 by Frank Barnwell, which first flew on 12 April 1935, following a 1934 order for one aircraft by Lord Rothermere. Wowed by the aircraft's high speed of 307 mph, which was considerably faster than the single-engine fighters of the time, the British Air Ministry was enthusiastic about the aircrafts potential as a bomber, and the aircraft, named 'Britain First', was turned over to the Air Ministry for evaluation.

With the Air Ministry showing an interest in the military potential of the aircraft various designs were drawn up for a bomber conversion capable of carrying a 1,000 lb. bomb load with a range of around 1,000 miles. The Bristol Mercury engine was selected over the rival Aquila and a design was drawn up for a three crew monoplane twin-engine medium bomber, which differed from the Type 142 in many respects. Most notable changes being provision for a Browning .303 in machine gun in the nose section which also accommodated a bomb aimer station. The aircraft's wings were raised some 16 inches, which was required to allow internal carriage of bombs. This alteration moved the new design to more a mid-wing rather than a low-wing monoplane; the Type 142 being described as the latter. A partially retractable mid-upper dorsal gun turret was provided just aft of the aircraft trailing edge, this initially being described fallaciously as an enclosed rear-gun turret. As with the main wing, the tail-plane and elevators were raised, the increase being about 8 inches, and span was increased. The aircraft was strengthened for its military role and all civil fixtures such as passenger windows were removed. The new military variant was allocated the company designation Type 142M as it still retained much commonality with the Type 142 from which it was clearly derived.

The Blenheim prototype, K7033, in 1936. The aircraft's high speed, for the time, showed much promise, although it would be outclassed by the new generation of monoplane fighters then under development in Britain and Germany. Air Ministry/MAP

Following a conference held in July 1935, at which time the above outline proposal was drawn up, the Air Ministry issued Specification 28/35 and authorized Bristol to proceed with design work. In September that year an order for 150 aircraft was placed off the drawing board, while foreign interest in the aircraft began to emerge from Finland and Lithuania. The aircraft was apparently named Blenheim in summer 1936, the production model being designated MK.I.

The prototype, K7033, conducted its maiden flight on 25 June 1936. Further flights were followed by service trials at Martlesham Heath which cleared the aircraft for production go-ahead in December that year, albeit with a number of changes incorporated. The first batch of Blenheim MK.I's, serials K7034 - K7182, were equipped with a B.I MK.I turret with only a single Lewis Machine gun, deliveries of these aircraft commencing in March 1937; No.114 Squadron at RAF Wyton being the first to equip with the type. The turrets were later replaced with B.I MK.III turrets housing a Vickers K machine gun, some aircraft being equipped with the MK.IIIA turret with two Vickers K's, although the Blenheim MK.IF fighters would enter service equipped with the MK.III turret with a single Vickers K machine Gun.

The prototype Blenheim, K7033, at Martlesham Heath during service evaluation in late 1936. Air Ministry/MAP

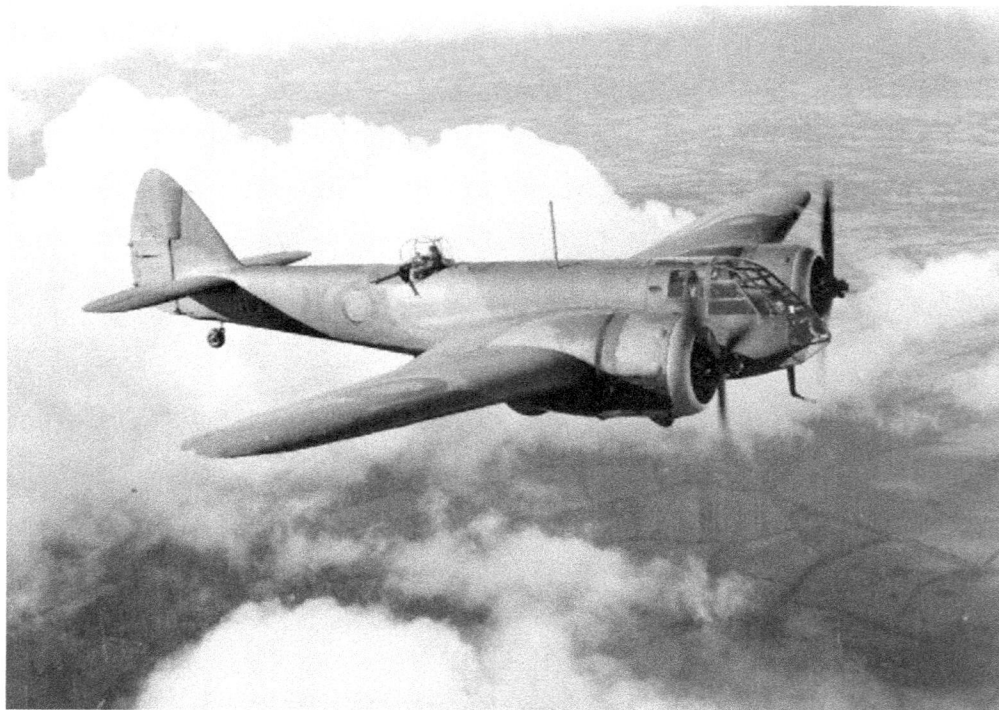

Blenheim MK.I, L1295, in flight pre-war. This aircraft was delivered to No.107 Squadron in August 1938, but was converted to a MK.IF in which guise it served with No.600 Squadron. RAF

The Blenheim MK.IF was basically a Blenheim I bomber modified by fitment of a battery of four .303 in Browning machine guns housed in a self-contained pack below the bomb bay; as noted above the aircraft retained the standard Vickers K machine gun armament for the mid-upper dorsal turret.

Further orders followed the initial order for 150 aircraft; 434 aircraft being ordered with serials L1097 - L1530, being added to by an additional 134 aircraft with serials L1531 - L1546 and L4817 - L4934. Once the urgent requirements for the RAF had been filled limited export orders were authorized to Finland, Turkey and Yugoslavia. Some 1,457 Blenheim MK.I's were produced; some 200 of these being subsequently converted to MK.IF standard for Fighter and Coastal Commands as MK.I airframes became available following the introduction of the Blenheim MK.IV bomber. A fighter conversion of the Blenheim MK.IV emerged as the MK.IVF, which served mainly with Coastal Command, although small numbers also served with Fighter Command alongside the MK.IF.

2

BLENHEIM MK.IF SQUADRONS

By the time of the Munich Crisis in late summer 1938 the RAF had no less than sixteen Blenheim bomber squadrons in service As war clouds were gathering over Europe in 1939, the Blenheim MKI was superseded in the bomber role in the European theatre by the Blenheim MK.IV, although the MK.I would still serve in the bomber role in the Mediterranean, Middle East and Far East.

With the availability of surplus Blenheim MK.I airframes following the introduction of the Blenheim MK.IV bomber, the RAF embarked upon a modest conversion of some 200 MK.I's to MK.IF standard. These twin-engine fighters would form the cutting edge of the RAF's small night fighter force, although the squadrons would also fly daylight operations, including shipping protection and long-range fighter sweeps. The first squadrons to re-equip with the Blenheim MK.IF were No's 23, 25 and 29 Squadrons, all receiving Blenheim's in winter 1938. As the last days of peace counted down in August 1939, the RAF had no less than seven Blenheim MK.IF fighter squadrons in service or converting with Fighter and Coastal Commands.

Formed at Fort Grange on 1 September 1915, No.23 Squadron served as a fighter squadron through World War 1 until it was disbanded towards the end of 1919, re-forming as a fighter unit on 1 July 1925. During the interwar period the squadron was equipped with various bi-plane fighters before receiving Blenheim IF monoplanes in winter 1938. Following the outbreak of war with Germany the squadron was tasked primarily as a night fighter unit, but also flew day patrols.

Formed from a nucleus of personnel from No.6 Reserve Squadron at Montrose, Scotland, on 25 September 1915, No.25 Squadron served through World War 1, being disbanded in January 1920, before re-forming some three months later. On 28 August 1938 the squadron re-equipped with Gloster

Gladiator single-seat bi-plane fighters for a short period, receiving the first Blenheim's on 10 December 1938; re-equipment being completed on 10 February 1939. The squadron began flying night patrols following the outbreak of war with Germany. Day fighter attacks on the German Sea-Plane base at Borkum were flown in November 1939, breaking the monotony of night patrols and day convoy escort patrols.

No.25 Squadron Blenheim IF's at Martlesham Heath in summer 1940. The belly gun pack can be seen on the nearest aircraft, which has also been equipped with AI MK III equipment for the night fighter role. RAF

Formed from an element of No.23 Squadron, No.29 Squadron was established as a fighter unit at Gosport on 7 November 1915; serving through World War 1, being disbanded on 31 December 1919, reforming again as a fighter squadron at Duxford on 1 April 1923. The squadron flew several types of single-seat fighters until it received Hawker Demon two-seat fighters in March 1935, before re-equipping with Blenheim IF's in December 1938.

No.64 Squadron was formed on 1 August 1916, operating on the western front from October 1917, disbanding on 31 December 1919. The squadron reformed at Heliopolis, Egypt, on 1 March 1936 and operated Hawker Demons before moving to Britain in August 1936, receiving Blenheim IF fighters at Church Fenton in late 1938. When war broke out in December 1939 the Blenheim's were used to conduct patrols off the East Coast. In December the squadron provided fighter defence for the Home Fleet from Evanton, Scotland, this posting lasting into January 1940. From April 1940 the squadron commenced conversion to Supermarine Spitfire single engine fighters.

As well as equipping operational squadrons some Blenheim MK.IF's equipped OTU's (Operational Training Units) such as No.17 OTU located at Upwood in the Midland's, probably the unit and location of this Blenheim MK.IF, L1359, WR-W, during 1940. RAF

No.600 (City of London) Squadron RAuxAF (Royal Auxiliary Air Force) was formed as a day bomber squadron at RAF Northolt on 14 October 1925, equipping with de Havilland DH.9A's and Avro 504N's. The squadron switched to the fighter role in July 1934, still equipped with Westland Wapitis, which it had received in 1929; Hawker Hart's being received in January 1935 while the squadron awaited re-equipment with Hawker Demon fighters; conversion to this type being completed in April 1937. The Demons were replaced by Bristol Blenheim IF fighters in January 1939.

When war was declared on Germany on 3 September 1939 the squadron was tasked with flying day and night fighter patrols as a counter to German raiders and reconnaissance aircraft. From December 1939, No.600 Squadron was also involved in experimental flights with Blenheim's equipped with AI (Airborne Interception) radar sets as the RAF strived towards introducing a viable operational radar to its small night fighter force.

Blenheim MK.IF's of No.25 Squadron at Martlesham Heath in July 1940. By this time the Blenheim was operating almost entirely in the night fighter role, aircraft ZK-X being equipped with AI MK.III radar equipment. RAF

Top: L6798 heads a line of No.604 Squadron Blenheim MK.IF's at RAF Northolt in April 1940. Above: The Blenheim IF turret housed a single .303 in Vickers K machine gun as on this Blenheim from No.245 Squadron. RAF

Top: This Blenheim MK.IF, L1336, WR-E, at RAF Northolt is from Hendon based No.248 Squadron. Above: Like the Blenheim MK.I, a number of Blenheim MK.IV's were converted to MK.IVF fighter configuration by addition of a belly gun pack. Some Blenheim IF squadrons converted to the MK.IVF after being transferred from Fighter to Coastal Command. This MK.IVF, N8239, WR-L, is from No.248 Squadron at North Coates, Lincolnshire. RAF

No.601 (County of London) Squadron RAuxAF formed at Northolt on 14 October 1925 as a light bomber squadron, but transferred to the fighter role on 1 July 1934, still equipped with Hawker Hart light bombers, which had been received in 1933. The Harts were replaced by Hawker Demons in August 1937, the squadron then converting to Gloster Gauntlet single-seat fighters in November 1938 before re-equipping with Blenheim IF fighters in January 1939. The Squadron operated Blenheim's until March 1940 when it re-equipped with Hawker Hurricane MK.I single-engine fighters.

Formed as a day bomber unit at RAF Hendon on 17 March 1930, No.604 (County of Middlesex) Squadron RAuxAF received the first of its allocation of DH.9A's on 2 April, but re-equipped with Wapitis in September that year. In September 1934 it switched to the fighter role, being re-equipped with Hawker Hart's for a short period until it received Hawker Demon fighters in June 1935. In 1939, the squadron re-equipped with Blenheim fighters and following the outbreak of war with Germany in September that year it flew defensive day and night patrols as well as conducting experimental flights with AI equipment.

Formed at Westgate, from seaplane units at Westgate and Manston, in August 1918, No.219 Squadron was disbanded on 7 February 1919. The squadron reformed at Catterick on 4 October 1939 as a Blenheim IF fighter squadron. Tasked with a shipping protection role, the squadron was declared operational on 21 February 1940 and then began to specialise in night patrols, deploying detachments to various locations. The squadron operated in the night fighter role through the summer and autumn months and commenced conversion to Bristol Beaufighters in winter 1940.

Formed at Thasos on 1 April 1918, No.222 Squadron operated against the Turks for the remainder of World War I, disbanding on 15 May 1919. The squadron reformed at Duxford on 5 October 1939 as a Blenheim IF fighter squadron, tasked with shipping protection. In March 1940 the squadron converted to Spitfire's.

Formed at Great Yarmouth on 20 August 1918, No.229 Squadron was employed on coastal patrols for the last few months of World War I, being disbanded on 31 December 1919. The squadron reformed as a fighter unit at Digby on 6 October 1939. Equipped with Blenheim IF's, the squadron was tasked primarily with shipping protection, operational patrols commencing on 21 December 1939. The squadron had a secondary night patrol role, conducting training flights and evaluation flights of aircraft fitted with AI equipment. In March 1940 the squadron re-equipped with Hawker Hurricane's.

Formed as a fighter squadron on 1 September 1917, No.92 Squadron moved to France in July 1918 for operations on the western front, disbanding on 7 August 1919. The squadron reformed at Tangmere on 10 October 1939 as a Blenheim IF fighter unit before converting to Spitfires in March 1940.

Formed at Aboukir (half-strength fighter squadron) on 15 May 1918, No.145 Squadron, equipped with SE.5A's, moved to Palestine in August that year, where it flew operations against Turkish forces, disbanding on 2 September 1919. The squadron reformed at Croydon on 10 October 1939, Blenheim's being received from December that year. After a short period flying Blenheim's the squadron commenced re-equipment with Hawker Hurricane's in March 1940.

No.233 Squadron reformed at Tadmere on 18 May 1937 as a GR (General Reconnaissance) Squadron equipped with Avro Anson's. The squadron converted to Lockheed Hudson's in August 1939, coastal patrols being flown by both types during the first weeks of World War II; the Anson's flying their last patrol on 10 October. At the end of October 1939, a Flight of Blenheim's was added to the squadron's strength, these being used to fly patrols until January 1940 when the flight was moved to Bircham Newton where it would form the nucleus of No.235 Squadron.

No.234 Squadron reformed as a Fighter Command squadron at Leconfield on 30 October 1939, initially tasked with protecting shipping, operating a disparate mix of Fairey Battle light bombers, Gloster Gauntlet bi-plane fighters and Blenheim IF long-range fighters, until March 1940, when the squadron re-equipped with Supermarine Spitfires.

No.235 Squadron had initially formed from No.'s 424 and 425 Flights at Newlyn, Cornwall, as a seaplane unit in August 1918 before disbanding on 22 February the following year. The squadron was re-formed on 30 October 1939 at Manston, Kent, initially operating Fairey Battle light bombers for training before receiving Blenheim's in December that year. Initially allocated to Fighter Command, the squadron was transferred to RAF Coastal Command on 27 February 1940, tasked with a long-range fighter and reconnaissance role. From May 1940 the squadron received some Blenheim MK.IVF's, a fighter conversion from Blenheim IV bombers, which were initially operated alongside the MK.IF.

Following the German invasion of Holland on 10 May the squadron flew reconnaissance missions, mainly searching for German naval units that, it was feared, could have attempted to seize the channel ports.

No.245 (Northern Rhodesian) Squadron formed as a Sea Plane unit from No's 426 and 427 Flights at Fishguard in August 1918 and was disbanded on 10 May 1919. The squadron re-formed at Leconfield on 30 October 1939 as a Blenheim fighter squadron, however, it was soon decided to equip the squadron with Hurricane single engine fighters, which began arriving in March 1940.

Formed from No's 404, 405 and 453 Sea plane Flights at Hornsea Meme in August 1918, No.248 Squadron flew coastal patrols in the closing months of World War I, disbanding on 6 March 1919. The squadron reformed at RAF Hendon as a Blenheim IF squadron on 30 October 1939. Tasked primarily with night patrols, after receiving Blenheim IF's in December 1939, the squadron was transferred from Fighter Command to Coastal Command at the end of February 1940, exchanging its Blenheim IF's for Blenheim IVF's, before returning to Fighter Command on 22 May, being based at Dyce, Scotland, with a detachment at Montrose.

Initially formed in May 1918 from No's 492, 517 and 518 Flights at Prawle Point, No.254 Squadron flew coastal patrols for the last few months of World War 1 before being disbanded on 22 February 1919. The Squadron reformed at Stradishall on 30 October 1939 as a Blenheim IF fighter squadron with Fighter Command. From 29 January 1940 the squadron began flying coastal patrols off the East Coast of Britain, being transferred to Coastal Command in April 1940, subsequently re-equipping with Blenheim MK.IVF's, flying convoy protection patrols and reconnaissance missions.

No.236 Squadron reformed at Stradishall as a Fighter Command squadron on 31 October 1939; Blenheim IF's being received in December that year. Towards the end of February 1940 the squadron moved to North Coates and transferred to Coastal Command, but transferred back to Fighter Command in April when it moved to Speke from where the squadron flew convoy protection patrols over the English Channel during the bleak days of May and June 1940. On 4 July 1940 the squadron again transferred to Coastal Command, tasked with a fighter and reconnaissance role.

No.242 Squadron received Blenheim IF's in December 1939, but these were replaced by Hurricanes the following month.

By May 1940 no less than 20 squadrons had operated Blenheim MK.IF's, many of these operating the type briefly until they were replaced by more capable fighters in the shape of Hawker Hurricane MK.I and Supermarine Spitfire MK.I's. Some of the squadrons operated with both Fighter Command and Coastal Command, and, in a few cases the MK.IF's were operated alongside MK.IVF's. Other units such as OTU (Operational Training Units) and the AFDU (Air Fighting Development Unit) also operated Blenheim IF's.

3

BLENHEIM MK.IF OPERATIONS - SEPTEMBER 1939 - 30 JUNE 1940

With the outbreak of war in September 1939, the RAF's Bristol Blenheim MK.IF fighter squadrons settled into the mundane routine of coastal patrols, convoy escorts, night patrols and training. This routine was occasionally interrupted by more active operations such as the raid on Borkum in November 1939.

No.25 Squadron, based at Hawkinge, had moved to take up a station at Northolt just before the declaration of war on 3 September 1939. The Squadron was primarily tasked with the night fighter role equipped with Blenheim IF's. However, an "experimental" Flight of four Blenheim MK.IVF fighters, with A.I. (Airborne Interception) radar fitted, had been attacked to the squadron since the 30th of August.

The squadron moved to Filton from 15 September until 4 October to fly cover patrols for the BEF (British Expeditionary Force) deploying to France, losing one Blenheim IF, L6678, which crashed while attempting to land following an engine failure. Two of the squadrons Blenheim IVF's were moved to Martlesham Heath on 22 November, from where they were to fly night patrols over the North Sea.

The first major operation for the Blenheim Fighter squadrons took place on 26 November 1939 when No.25 Squadron was tasked with conducting an attack on the German Sea plane base at Borkum Island off the coast of Saxony, North West Germany. The aim of the attack was to disrupt the German Sea Plane minelaying operations. Nine Blenheim's, L1437 (S/Ldr. A.R. Hallings-Pott/P/O Verese/AC Scrase), L1440 (F/O Lyall/AC McCarthy), L1408 (Sgt. Haine/AC Bignell), L6676 (F/Lt. Bull/P/O Ensor/AC McCormack), L6736 (F/O Walker/AC Strode), L1406 (P/O Miley/AC Mortimer), L1433 (F/Lt. Cave/Sgt. Hawken/AC Rolls), L1426 (F/O Burke/AC Bromme and L6677 (F/O Emmett/AC Hine), took off from Northolt at 11.15 hours in very rough weather (S.W. gale/65-70 mph winds) which was encountered during the entire mission. The aircraft crossed over water near to Yarmouth and set course for the Terschelling Lightship at 11.45 hours. About 15 minutes later one of the Blenheim's, L1426, F/O Burke/AC Bromme, suffered engine trouble and subsequently returned to Northolt on one engine. The remaining eight aircraft were unable to locate the Terschelling Lightship or the German or Dutch coasts at the planned estimated time of arrival; 12.28 hours. The formation continued on its course for a further ten minutes, following which two course alternations were made in an attempt to find land. About 13.03 hours the formation had still not made landfall and it was decided to abort the mission and return to Northolt, flying at 500 - 1,000 ft., landfall being made some 8 miles north of Yarmouth at 14.25 hours; the aircraft landing at Northolt at 13.05 hours. It was later determined that the Blenheim's had turned for home when about 30 miles N.N.W. of Borkum Island.

The above mission had been in inauspicious start to the Blenheim IF's first daylight fighter sweep over enemy territory. Undeterred by the failure of the previous operation, Fighter Command scheduled another operation against Borkum for the 28th, this time the mission would be flown by one Flight of six aircraft from 25 Squadron and a Flight of 6 aircraft from 601 Squadron at Biggin Hill. Both Flights departed base and landed at Bircham Newton to refuel.

The six Blenheim's from 25 Squadron, L1437 (S/Ldr. Hallings-Pott/Sgt. Hawken/AC Scrase), L1408 (Sgt. Haine/Sgt. Belfitt/AC Bignell), L1440 (F/O Lyall/Sgt. Baker/AC McCarthy), L6676 (F/Lt. Bull/P/O Ensor/AC Mortimer), L1433 (P/O Walker/Sgt. Battle/AC Strode) and L1406 (P/O Miley/Sgt. Boner/AC Taylor), took off from Bircham Newton at 14.05 hours in company with six Blenheim's, L8701, L6617, L6722, L6880, L6720 and L6605 from 601 Squadron; S/Ldr. Hallings-Pott from 25 Squadron in command.

The 25 Squadron narrative for the operation is reproduced below verbatim:

"Squadron ordered to carry out a low-flying machine-gun attack on BORKUM Seaplane Base, in conjunction with 601 Squadron. One flight (6 aircraft) of each squadron left NORTHOLT 1130 hours to refuel at BIRCHAM NEWTON. Took off again at 14.05 hours on course for ENGESHAMS GAT, which was reached at 15.09 hours. Altered course for BORKUM and arrived over objective 1525 hours, coming out of rainstorm at 1,000 ft. below cloud. First saw island at West Corner, turned South very low and approximately 4 miles from coast and made run into Seaplane Base down a wind of 40 - 50 m.p.h. Four sections attacked in quick succession in echelon port formations.

1st Section – S/LDR. J.R. HALLINGS-POTT, F/O. A.M. LYALL, SGT. R.C. HAINE) approached up mole and machine-gunned one seaplane on slipway in basin, attacked and passed over hangers and attacked three seaplanes on slipway on other side of peninsular. Turned

off East and South passing over grey ship.

2nd Section – 601 Squadron.

3rd Section – F/LT. C.H. BUL, F/O. J.H.G. WALKER, P/O. M.J. MILEY) attacked seaplane in corner of basin, cleared gun position on corner of hanger. One pilot turned sharply and passed through gap in mole (F/O. WALKER). Hangers machine-gunned and ship fired on, on turn South and West.

4th Section – 601 Squadron.

Squadron left BORKUM at 1531 hours and reformed for flight home. Navigation lights were switched on ten minutes after leaving BORKUM and return flight was carried out in darkness. All twelve machines landed at Debden at 1755 hours. No hits were found on machines."

The No.601 Squadron narrative of the operation is reproduced below verbatim:

27 November 1939: "Three Aircraft from 'A' Flight (Blenheim's No. L.8701, L.6617, L.6722) and three aircraft from 'B' Flight (Blenheim's No. L.6880, L.6720 and L.6605) left Biggin Hill for Northolt at 14.44 hours. On arrival at Northolt, the pilots received orders to participate in a projected raid on the German seaplane-base at BORKUM the following day. Crews of aircraft, wireless personnel, and armourers arrived at Northolt shortly after, and spent the entire night equipping the aircraft for the operation."

28 November 1939: "The equipment was completed by 10.30 hours on 28.11.39. Six navigators and three Wireless Operators (Air Crew) joined the detachment, and together with three Wireless Operators (Air Crew) and 6 pilots from 601 Squadron, completed the crews of the six aircraft. The aircraft took off in company with six aircraft of No.25 Squadron at 11.30 hours and flew to Bircham Newton.

The 12 aircraft left Bircham Newton at 14.15 hours, flying in four sections led by Squadron Leader Pott; Flight Lieutenant M.F. Peacock leading the second section, and Flying Officer M. Aitken leading the fourth section.

Front gun attacks were made at BORKUM at 15.25 hours by all aircraft, which returned immediately, and made landfall at Great Yarmouth at 17.05. It was then decided to follow 25 Squadron back to Northolt, and not to return to Manston as had originally been intended.

At 17.50 the formation arrived at Debden, and Squadron Leader Pott decided to land there, and all aircraft landed successfully.

There was no injury to personnel or damage to aircraft. 3,622 rounds had been fired (3,600 from front guns, 22 from rear guns), and one gun alone out of 36, experienced a stoppage."

The above mission, led By S/Ldr. Hallam-Potts of No.25 Squadron, was lauded in the press as a major success, causing much damage to the German base. However, subsequent findings would later show that the mission inflicted only light damage, despite, which, it was successfully planned and executed without casualties to the attacking force.

On the 29th, the Blenheim's from 601 and 25 Squadron took off from Debden at 10.30 and returned to Northolt. The six No.601 Squadron aircraft took off from Northolt at 12.30 hours and flew to Biggin Hill where they landed at 13.00 hours.

No.25 Squadron was ordered to conduct a 'North Sea Sweep' on 7 December, but this was cancelled due to adverse weather. The sweep was rescheduled for 10 December, six Blenheim MK.IF's, codes ZK-P, ZK-R, ZK-Q, ZK-A, ZK-B and ZK-O, taking off from Northolt at 09.50 hours. The Flight crossed the coast at North Foreland then came onto course 90 degrees for a period of 10 minutes, 40 degrees for 40 minutes, 265 degrees for 40 minutes, before re-crossing the coast at the area of Cromer, landing at Northolt at 12.35 hours; no enemy forces having been encountered.

Another 'North Sea Sweep' was scheduled for take-off at 07.30 hours on the morning of 14 December, but the patrol was cancelled due to adverse weather. The squadron conducted no more sweep operations during 1939, a move to North Weald being conducted on 20 January 1940. On 10 February 1940, No.25 Squadron detached six Blenheim IF's, codes ZK-P, ZK-Q, ZK-O, ZK-S, ZK-L and ZK-N, to Martlesham Heath, from where they were to fly as escort to a "Naval convoy to Dutch coast and back" the following day. However, on arrival at Martlesham Heath the squadron was told that the operation had actually been cancelled some 3 days previous.

In the months following, the Blenheim squadrons settled into a routine of occasional patrols and training flights; a routine that would befall the remaining Blenheim fighter squadrons through the early months of 1940. Shipping protection and coastal patrols were conducted by a number of Blenheim squadrons from Fighter and Coastal Commands, some of the Blenheim squadron having been formed specifically for this task.

There were few encounters with enemy aircraft, but No.604 Squadron had an engagement with a He.111 on 29 January 1940 and a Section of No.254 Squadron Blenheim's were engaged in a prolonged dog-fight with a He.111 on 22 February 1940.

The Combat Report for the No.254 Squadron attack on the He.111 is reproduced below verbatim. **Note:** Some reports suggest that No.254 Squadron transferred from Fighter Command to Coastal Command in April 1940, however, the following Combat Report originates from Coastal Command, which, along with other operational records imply that the squadron transferred to Coastal Command in February 1940 and converted to MK.IVF's in April.

COMBAT REPORT – BLENHEIMS "Q", "N", "R", 254 SQUADRON – 22nd February, 1940.

Blenheims "Q", "N" and "R" were in company on a track of 90° at 2000 feet when a Heinkel 111 was sighted in position VLAA 0015 flying on a course of 300° T at about 1500 feet, at 1214 hours on 22nd February. The He.111 had the elliptical wing plan characteristic of the earlier types and a lower gun position. This lower gun appeared to have a canvas cover and was not used during the action. The aircraft appeared to be camouflaged a greyish brown colour generally.

The Blenheims altered course to get on the tail of the enemy aircraft, which took avoiding action by diving down almost to sea level and executing "S" turns.

Narrative of Attack.

The Blenheims made a series of shallow dive attacks astern and abeam of the enemy aircraft and fired bursts at ranges from 500 to 200 yards. Several bursts were fired by rear gunners during the engagement. In all 6348 rounds were expended by the Blenheims during the attack.

Effect of Attack.

Several bursts were seen to enter the fuselage of the enemy aircraft, but no apparent damage was inflicted and when all the ammunition had been expended by the Blenheims the enemy aircraft disappeared in an easterly direction.

One of our aircraft had one or two bullet holes in wings and another was struck by 5 bullets, including one which struck between two cylinders of an engine.

Particulars of Heinkel's Armament.

The enemy aircraft had only one front gun, which appeared to be free, one gun in the upper gun position and one in the lower gun position, this latter being in a fixed cupola. The enemy aircraft was firing approximately 1 in 4 tracer or incendiary.
While the Blenheims were approaching the enemy aircraft the latter fired a white-white Very's light. In manoeuvre, the Blenheims found

themselves able to turn inside the Heinkel.

In amplification of paragraphs 2, 3 and 4, it is stated that:-

(i)   The Blenheims tried to get on the tail of the enemy aircraft but before they were able to do so the enemy aircraft began a turn to starboard and continued to turn and lose height until it had reached a height of only 100 feet above sea level.

(ii)   The Blenheims then tried to get on to the tail of the enemy aircraft in order to make no-deflection astern attack but were unable to do so as the enemy aircraft never held a straight course for any appreciable length of time.

(iii)   At one period of the combat, the enemy aircraft executed a tight turn for 3-4 minutes on end; during this time the Blenheims were able to get in some good full deflection shots from ranges of 400 yards down to 200 yards.

(iv)   It was not possible to haul off for a dive attack owing to the poor visibility and fear of losing contact with the enemy; the combat therefore developed into a prolonged dog-fight during which all four aircraft were never more than a mile apart.

(v)   On the occasions on which the fighters broke off from the turn the rear gunners were able to get some good shots in.

(vi)   After 12 minutes the leader ran out of front gun ammunition and endeavoured to give his rear gunner a shot by pulling out of tight turns close to the enemy aircraft, the other two aircraft meanwhile pressing home front gun attacks whenever an opportunity presented itself.

(vii)   The observer of the leading aircraft noted tracer bullets entering the fuselage of the enemy aircraft about the nose and centre section during the deflection shooting.

(viii) The leader fired 7 bursts in all, one of which was a particularly long burst as he had been able to get a good aim.

                                (Signed)
                                     For Wing Commander,
                        Senior Intelligence Officer,
                        HEADQUARTERS COASTAL COMMAND,
8th March, 1940   ROYAL AIR FORCE.

Routine patrols was the remit of most Blenheim fighters squadrons as the period known as the 'Phony War' was fast coming to its conclusion. For the most part these patrols encountered nothing, but occasionally the monotony was broken, such as on 10 April 1940 when a No.25 Squadron Blenheim IF, flying a convoy escort patrol, reported observing an aircraft which resembled a German He.111 bomber. The aircraft was observed fleetingly at a range of 600 yards before being lost in cloud.

On 23 April, Blenheim L8657 of No.25 was damaged by British anti-aircraft fire while on a night patrol. During another patrol that night the crew of Blenheim K7113 observed an enemy aircraft "momentarily against the moon, but unidentified." A No.219 Blenheim IF had an encounter with enemy aircraft on 3 May 1940. Following the German invasion of Norway, Coastal Command Blenheim fighters flew operations against German forces in Norway.

As the anticipated German Blitzkrieg against the Low Countries and France commenced in the early morning of 10 May 1940 the Allied Armies massed on the Franco-Belgian border put into operation Plan 'D' (Dyle); the move into Belgium to meet the German advance, as the Germans were punching deep into Belgium and Holland through ground and airborne operations. In line with previous doctrine the RAF units in France were reinforced.

When the hammer fell on Holland in the early morning of 10 May the Dutch had some initial success in frustrating German airborne assaults against such centers as the Hague, but these would be temporary in nature as the German attack had secured many vital objectives, including airfields, which included Ypenburg aerodrome near the Hague. The Dutch accordingly requested British assistance, including the requirement for the RAF to operate over Holland, which was the real crisis area on this first day of the campaign known as the Blitzkrieg; the Dutch air force having been all but annihilated in the initial German onslaught, and while some Dutch units were able to continue putting aircraft into the air, the air force was to all intents and purposes destroyed as an effective fighting force on that first day of battle.

Ground attack operations were flown by Blenheim MK.IF twin-engine fighters of No.600 Squadron Fighter Command on the 10th, followed by a later attack by Blenheim Bombers; the Blenheim fighters suffering heavily, with five out of a formation of six that had attacked Waalhaven being shot down by German Me.110 twin-engine fighters. No.604 Squadron later attacked Junker Ju-52 transport aircraft that had landed troops on beaches near The Hague.

Over the next few days Fighter Command Spitfires, Hurricanes and the Defiant's of No.264 Squadron flew many sorties over Holland, particularly over The Hague, while RAF bombers continued to attack targets, including aerodromes; but the inexorable tide of the German advance was such that little could be done to slow it, let alone stop it, and Holland accordingly capitulated on 15 May.

For No.600 Squadron May 1940 had commenced with the continuation of training flights, interrupted by handfuls of mundane escort patrols. On 2 May a few escort patrols were flown, two more "train ferry" escort patrols being flown on the 6th, a convoy escort and a "train ferry" escort being flown on the 7th and convoy and "train ferry" escorts being flown on the 8th.

No.600 Squadron operations on 10 May 1940 commenced before the German invasion of Holland. The squadron's first combat of the day commenced around 05.00 hours when a Blenheim IF, which had taken off on patrol at 03.40 hours, intercepted a Luftwaffe He.111 bomber.

No.600 Squadrons narrative of this encounter with He.111's in the early morning of 10 May 1940 is reproduced below verbatim:

"At 0340 PILOT OFFICER ANDERSON was sent off on patrol and was vectored towards France after "Bogey". On giving up the search for "Bogey" he climbed to regain R/T touch and sighted an HE 111 flying across his course about 2000 feet below him flying W.S.W. at approximately 160 mph. He prepared to take up No.1 attack when another HE 111 was reported by his gunner flying behind him, so he turned and attacked it, at the same time his gunner reported four more aircraft flying in box formation out of range behind him. Before Pilot Officer Anderson opened fire the rear gunner of the HE.111 opened accurate fire at about 600 yards range; closing to about 400 yards, PILOT OFFICER ANDERSON fired until his ammunition was exhausted and some tracers were seen to enter the enemy aircraft. Then he flew below the He.11 (He.111) to enable his gunner L.A.C. BAKER to fire at about 100 yards range. The gunner appeared to be out of action and PILOT OFFICER ANDERSON broke off the engagement dived to sea level and returned to MANSTON, when he found that the hydraulic system had been put out of action by a bullet and he had land without the aid of undercarriage or flaps. This he did successfully. Several bullet holes were observed in the aircraft one through the port tank, one through the back of the pilots seat and one on the port airscrew. The rear gunners turret was put out of action and also the R/T. early in the engagement but neither occupant was injured."

The No.600 Squadron Fighter Command Combat Report for the combat with a Heinkel 111 early on the morning of 10 May 1940 is reproduced below verbatim:

FORM 'F'.

FIGHTER COMMAND COMBAT REPORT.

To:-   Fighter Command

From:- 11 Group

(A)	Sector Serial No.	
(B)	Serial No. of detailing Flight or Squadron to patrol.	
(C)	Date	10.5.40.
(D)	Flight 'B' Green 1 Squadron 600	
(E)	Number of Enemy Aircraft	6
(F)	Type of Enemy Aircraft	He.111KV
(G)	Time attack was delivered	About 0500 hours.
(H)	Place attack was delivered	20 miles N.W. Cape Gris Nez.
(J)	Height of enemy	7,000 ft. approx.
(K)	Enemy Casualties	Unknown
(L)	Our Casualties	Aircraft Nil.
		Personnel Nil.
(N)	(i) Searchlights (did they illuminate enemy, if not, were they in front or behind target)	N/A
	(ii) Anti-aircraft guns (did shell bursts assist pilot in intercepting the enemy)	N/A
(P)	Range at which fire was opened in each attack on enemy together with estimated length of burst 400 – 500 yds. 2,400 rounds	3 bursts of 8 secs.

(R)   **GENERAL REPORT**.

Good visibility, no cloud; at 1,000 ft. Green 1 whilst on patrol was vectored across channel towards France after Bogey. On giving up search for Bogey he climbed to regain R/T touch and sighted 1 He.111 flying across his course about 2,000 ft. below, flying S.W. at approx. 160 m.p.h. He prepared to take up No.1 attack when another He.111 was reported by his gunner flying behind him. Green 1 turned and attacked using No.1 attack; rear gunner observed 4 more aircraft flying in formation out of range behind Green 1. Before Green 1 opened fire and at about 600 yds. - 500 yds. Lower, rear gunner on He.111 opened accurate fire and bullets entered Green 1 machine. Green 1 opened fire at approx. 500 - 400 yds. and saw some tracers entering enemy aircraft. Having exhausted front ammunition Green 1 dived below, pulled up aside of e/a to within 100 yds. in order to give rear gunner opportunity of firing. Rear gunner appeared to be out of action and Green 1 broke off engagement dived to sea level and returned to base. Slight black smoke appeared to come from port engine of e/a but e/a did not appear to be in any trouble.

On arriving at base Green 1 found hydraulic system to be out of action and was forced to land without flaps or undercarriage. Three bullet holes observed, 1 in port petrol tank, 1 through pilots backrest of seat and 1 hitting port air screw. R/T system also put out of action early in engagement (Green 1 was slightly in front, approx. 100 yds. Below e/a the front gun of which shot at Green 1 but did not hit). Usual markings and camouflage.

Rec.   0853 hours,
10.5.40.

ANDERSON. P/O

On the morning of 10 May a section of three Blenheim fighters from No.235 Squadron Coastal Command conducted a patrol off the Dutch coast and Frisian Islands, no enemy forces being observed. It was Fighter Command and Bomber Command, however, that would conduct the major offensive operations over Holland on this date.

No.600 Squadron was ordered to conduct an attack on Rotterdam airport, which was in enemy hands after being captured earlier that day by German parachute troops; six Blenheim's taking off at 12.00 hours. A strafing attack was conducted on Luftwaffe Junkers Ju.52 transport aircraft on the aerodrome, immediately following which, the Blenheim's were in turn attacked by Me.110 long-range twin-engine fighters from 3/ZG.1.

The No.600 Squadron Narrative of the attack on Rotterdam aerodrome and subsequent patrols is reproduced below verbatim:

"At 1200 hours the COMMANDING OFFICER with FLYING OFFICERS MOORE, ROWE AND HAYES, and PILOT OFFICERS ANDERSON AND HAINE were sent off to attack ROTTERDAM aerodrome which had been taken by GERMAN parachute troops and to destroy any aircraft in the air or on the ground. Arriving there they dived over the aerodrome attacked and destroying a JU 82 (should read Ju.52) on the ground and climbing, were immediately attacked by 12 ME 110 which had apparently been patrolling above. There was a fierce fight the exact effects of which on the MEs cannot be stated as it is not certain how

much the rear gunners were able to fire.

FLYING OFFICER HAYES was very ably directed by CORPORAL HOLMES as to how and when to turn and succeeded in shaking off his pursuers. The machine was severely damaged in the starboard wing and the petrol tank was pierced. He made for home but almost immediately encountered 3 HE 111s which he immediately attacked with his remaining ammunition and succeeded in breaking up the formation before bringing his aircraft back safely. Neither the pilot nor the air gunner were wounded. The remaining five machines were reported missing… The crews of the missing were SQUADRON LEADER WELLS, CORPORAL KIDD (gunner) SERGEANT DAVIS (observer) PILOT OFFICER HAINE, PILOT OFFICER KRAMER (gunner), FLYING OFFICER ROWE, PILOT OFFICER ECHLIN (gunner), PILOT OFFICER ANDERSON, L.A.C. HAWKINS (Gunner) PILOT OFFICER MOORE CPL. ISAACS (gunner).”

Note: Various accounts of the above action imply, or at least lead the reader to infer, that the Blenheim's shot down one or more of the Me.110's, however, German operational records clearly show no Me.110 losses on any front during the operations of 10 May 1940. Although some accounts claim "several" Ju-52's destroyed, Squadron records claimed only one confirmed destroyed in the attack. There is also an account of one of the Blenheim's encountering and engaging a Me.109 which flew alongside the Blenheim; the Me.109 being stated to have possibly crashed. However, authentic Squadron and Command documents show no record of this and it has not been possible to tie it up to a German loss record. It is possible that the aircraft was Dutch, or simply the fog of war.

At 13.30 hours 'A' Flight of 600 Squadron took off to conduct a patrol of the Belgian coast. After almost an hour on patrol the Blenheim's encountered a He.111 in the air, which was then attacked by Red Section, the He.111 being chased up the Dutch coast by Red 2 and 3, claiming it damaged, before they disengaged from the chase due to Dutch anti-aircraft fire that also targeted the He.111, which was last seen diving towards the sea. Red Section reformed with the remainder of the Flight before turning for home.

The No.600 Squadron narrative of the patrol is detailed below verbatim:

"…at approximately 1330 hours "A" Flight, consisting of Flight Lieutenant CLARK, FLYING OFFICER CLACKSON, FLYING OFFICER SMITH and FLYING OFFICER HANNAY took off for a patrol of the Belgian cost from MIDDLELKECK to ZEEBRUGE. The sections were placed stepped up, one at 5,000 feet, one at 10,000 feet. The

day was cloudless and visibility excellent. After 55 minutes on the patrol line a HE 111 was sighted and RED section attacked. Fire was experienced by the leader just before the first burst, but after firing three bursts at it, no further bursts were experienced. RED two and three continued the attack and chased the aircraft up the Dutch coast. Approximately 4,000 rounds were fired at it altogether and many hits were observed. It was last seen diving towards the sea with considerable smoke pouring from it, hotly engaged by DUTCH anti-aircraft fire in which No.2 and 3 soon found themselves also. The section rejoined over MIDDELKECK and the flight left for home relived by No.25 Squadron."

'A' Flight conducted another patrol in the late afternoon, taking off at 17.00 hours to patrol a line Zeebrugge to Flushing. It has been erroneously stated in some accounts that the Flight strafed and destroyed a He.111 observed on the ground near Flushing. However, this is a fallacy; the Squadron and Fighter Command operational records clearly detailing that the He.111 encountered had already crashed. Other than the above mentioned wreck, the squadron encountered no other enemy aircraft and returned to base, landing at 19.30 hours.

The squadron narrative for the above patrol is reproduced below verbatim:

"In the afternoon at 1700 hours the flight went off again but was ordered to patrol the advanced line ZEEBRUGGE TO FLUSHING, but only friendly aircraft were encountered: a crashed HEINKEL was seen on the ground. The flight returned at 1930 hours. In the evening, three pilots went to HAWKINGE, BIGGEN HILL and GRAVESEND in case a special job was required of them, but they returned the next morning not having been called upon."

On 10 May No.25 Squadron was based between Martlesham Heath and North Weald. The squadron moved 11 Blenheim IF's to RAF Hawkinge, from where they flew fighter sweeps along the Belgian and Dutch coasts, in company with three more of the squadrons Blenheim's (Red Section), which operated from Martlesham Heath. The aim of the sweeps was to protect Allied Naval units tasked with blocking the entrances to a number of channel ports, which it was feared, could be seized by German forces.

The first patrol, which took off from Hawking at 14.15 hours, consisted of six Blenheim IF's coded ZK.-H (F/Lt. Bull/AC McCormack), ZK-K (F/O Walker/AC Bignell), ZK-B (F/O Miley/P/O Chapman), ZK-F (P/O Rofe/AC Taylor), ZK-J (P/O Howe/LAC Berwick) and ZK-I (Sgt. Smith/LAC Grose). The Patrol encountered no enemy aircraft and returned to base, landing at 16.35 hours. The second patrol, six Blenheim IF's coded ZK-O (F/Lt. Lyall/LAC

Austin), ZK-N (F/O Lambert/AC Rolls), ZK-U (F/O Haworth/LAC Cave), ZK-L (P/O Cassidy/AC Miller), ZK-Q (P/O Hooper/LAC Chiplin) and ZK-R (F/Sgt. Monk/LAC Bingley), took off at 15.30 hours and landed at 18.00 hours having not encountered any enemy. The squadrons third patrol of the day again consisted of six Blenheim IF's, coded ZK-H (S/Ldr. Macewen/AC McCormack), ZK-K (F/O Walker/AC Bignell), ZK-B (F/O Miley/P/O Chapman), ZK-F P/O Rofe/AC Taylor), ZK-J (P/O Howe/LAC Berwick) and ZK-I (Sgt. Smith/LAC Grose), which took off at 18.30 to patrol the Belgian and Dutch coasts, landing back at base at 20.45, having encountered no enemy forces.

On 10 May, No.604 was ordered to move 6 Blenheim IF's from Kenly to Wattisham from where they were later to fly as escort to Blenheim IV bombers of No.110 Squadron. The six aircraft, L9693 (F/Lt. Davies/Sgt. Brooke/ P/O Scott), L8675 (P/O Selway/AC Goodman), L1517 (P/O Joll/LAC Pickford), L6728 (P/O Doulton/LAC Nesbitt), L8715 (F/O Scott/LAC Penn) and L6723 (Sgt. McDonald/LAC Peirce), took off from Kenly at 15.05 hours and landed at Wattisham at 15.45 where they were turned around before taking off at 16.30 hours to rendezvous with No.110 Squadron which was to conduct an attack on German airborne forces around The Hague.

The report on the 604 Squadron attack on the beaches at The Hague is reproduced below verbatim:

COPY OF REPORT ON RAID ON BEACHES AT THE HAGUE.

10.5.40.

FORM F.   SECRET.

A B 1 A B 80 C 10/5/40   D B 604 E NIL   F JUNKERS 52 G 1735

H SCHEVENING   J MIL K 4 CERTAIN AND 3 PROBABLE L 1 BLENHEIM

M 2 MISSING   SEARCHLIGHTS (N1)   AAGUNS (N2) RANGE (F)

THIS REPORT COVERS THE ATTACKS OF THE 5 BLENHEIMS WHICH RETURNED FROM THE RAID.

(R)
B Flight left KENLEY at 1505 hours. Landed at WATTISHAM 1545 hours Refuelled and left at 1630 hours. Escorting 12 Long Nosed

Blenheim Bombers on a raid on a beach 8 miles North of THE HAGUE where enemy aircraft were known to have landed.

On reaching the DUTCH coast 3 ME110's were sighted about 3 miles from the formation but they turned away and were not seen again.

The formation reached its objective at 1735 and attacked 9 JU52's which were observed on the beach in a line. Two of these aircraft were set on fire in this stage of the attack. The bombers having completed their attack turned for home at 1740 hours.

B Flight then formed into sections line astern and attacked with their front guns. Blue section led the attack in a vertical dive from 5000 ft. followed by a shallow dive down the line of enemy aircraft machine gun fire was encountered from the rear guns of the Junkers and tracer was observed streaming past the tails of the first two BLENHEIMS.

No.3 was apparently hit and force landed on fire amongst the sand dunes. The pilot and air gunner appeared to be uninjured. Green Section followed with a similar attack but did not observe any return fire from the enemy aircraft although No.6 was damaged by an enemy bullet.

Green Section completed their attack and finally observed in addition to the 2 aircraft destroyed by the bombers, 4 had been set on fire and a further 3 severely damaged by our machine gun fire.

No troops were seen on the ground but a trench was observed close to the line of aircraft by one of the gunners. He saw nobody in the trench and no return fire was observed from it. The only opposition encountered was from the rear guns of the Junkers.

All pilots could see their bullet patterns clearly on the sand and passing through all the Junkers.

After all aircraft had attacked the five remaining BLENHEIMs returned at sea level and landed at WATTISHAM.

Blue Section at 1830 and Green Section at 1915

After refueling, 4 aircraft left WATTISHAM at 2010 and landed at KENLEY at 2055. One aircraft, No.6 was left at WATTISHAM as an enemy bullet had broken several pipes on the air pressure line.

The personnel engaged were as follows.
B Flight 604 Squadron
Blue Section Leader F/Lt J.A. DAVIES, P/O R. SCOTT, SGT. H.W. BROOK.
BLUE 2 P/O. J.B. SELWAY and LAC M. GOODMAN.
BLUE 3 P/O. I.K.S. JOLL and LAC J. PICKFORD.
GREEN Section Leader F/O. M.D. DOULTON and LAC NESBITT.
GREEN 2 F/O R.H. SCOTT and LAC PENN.
GREEN 3 SGT. A.S. McDONALD and LAC A.F. PEIRCE

Note: The Squadron Form 540 states that it was Me.109 single-engine fighters that were observed while en-route to the Dutch coast, although this was unlikely, it being more probable that the fighters were Me.110's.

After being hit, L1517, Blue 3, crash landed about 8 miles north of Scheveningen, Holland, at approximately 17.45 hours. The remaining five aircraft returned to Wattisham between 18.50 and 19.15 hours, where they refueled before taking off again at 20.10 hours bound for Kenley where they landed at 20.55 hours.

What the Blenheim 1F operations of 10 May had shown was that the aircraft was completely unsuitable for the day fighter role. The standard German long-range twin-engine fighter, the Me.110, had proven to be superior to the Blenheim, which was even more hopelessly outclassed by the Me.109 single-engine fighter. There would be no further daytime Blenheim fighter sweeps over Holland. However, the RAF continued to give offensive and defensive support to the Dutch, flying bombing missions from Britain and the continent as well as flying fighter sweeps with Hawker Hurricane MK.I, Supermarine Spitfire MK.I and Boulton Paul Defiant MK.I single-engine fighters of RAF Fighter Command. The inexorable tide of the German advance, however, could only be delayed, the Dutch inevitably capitulating on 15 May 1940. Following the capitulation the RAF continued to fly offensive operations over The Netherlands, targeting among other things enemy aerodromes.

On 11 May, No.25 Squadron flew a single squadron strength fighter sweep. Twelve Blenheim's, ZK-P (S/Ldr. Macewan/AC Scrase), ZK-O (F/O Lyall/P/O Poter), ZK-H (F/O Lambert/AC Rolls), ZK-Q (F/O Emmett/AC Kane), ZH-U (F/O Howarth/LAC Cave), ZK-L (F/Sgt. Monk/LAC Bingley), ZK-H (F/Lt. Bull/AC Mortimer), ZK-K (F/O Walker/AC Bignell), ZK-B (F/O Miley/P/O Chapman), ZK-V (P/O Rofe/AC Taylor), ZK-J (P/O Howe/LAC Berwick) and ZK-I (Sgt. Thompson/LAC Grose), took off at 14.15 hours with the same orders as the previous day; protection of Allied Naval units blockading the continental ports. The Squadron patrolled from Nieuport Bain northwards to Flushing where German dive bombers were observed attacking shipping. As the squadron approached the dive bombers left, having already conducted their attack. A Junkers Ju.88 and a Dornier Do.17 were observed, but the squadron did not make contact with either enemy aircraft, and returned to base, landing at 16.45 hours.

On the 12th No.25 Squadron again moved its aircraft to Hawkinge and was stood by to fly similar patrols to the previous two days. However, no orders to patrol were forthcoming and the squadron returned to North Weald where it was, according to the Form 540, learned "that R.D.F. plots had been received that morning of approximately 38 E.A. on the Squadrons patrol line at 15, 20, and 25 thousand feet." This cancellation of the Blenheim's patrols in the face of enemy aircraft was confirmation that the Blenheim's days as a day fighter with Fighter Command in the European Theatre were all, but over; the type being employed increasingly in the night fighter role coupled with a decreasing number of daytime local base patrols and naval and convoy escorts and the odd fighter sweep towards the end of the month.

On 14 May, No.25 Squadrons last operational sorties in support of the campaign in the Netherlands were undertaken when a two aircraft section escorted the Destroyer HMS *Versatile*, which was being escorted by the Destroyer HMS *Janus*. HMS *Versatile* had been damaged by a bombing attack by Luftwaffe aircraft off the Dutch coast whilst participating in the evacuation from that country. The two Blenheim's took over the air segment of the escort from three Coastal Command Lockheed Hudson's at 08.00 hours, with five Blenheim's conducting escort patrols at various periods throughout the day. There is no mention of the operation in the Squadrons Form 541, but it is detailed in the Form 540 and other operational records.

There were no operational flights by 600 Squadron on the 11th, and only a single operational sortie was flown on the 12th; a Blenheim being sent to intercept "an X raid" failing to make contact. On the 13th the squadron received orders to move to Northolt, being relieved at Manston by No.604 Squadron; 'B' Flight moving the following day, followed by 'A' Flight on the 15th.

On the 12th and 13th of May 'B' Flight No.604 Squadron conducted shipping escort patrols from Northolt. On the 14th 'B' Flight moved to Manston and was operational by 13.00 hours, later conducting shipping escort patrols. The following day 'A' Flight joined 'B' Flight at Manston, being operational by 13.00 hours. 'B' Flight flew shipping escort patrols from Manston on the 15th and the squadron embarked upon a night flying program, sorties being flown between 23.00 hours on the 15th and 00.30 hours on the 16th. On 18 May 'A' Flight No.604 Squadron was ordered to move to Hawkinge, the move being completed by 19.30 hours that evening.

As well as Fighter Commands Blenheim IF's, Coastal Command Blenheim IVF long-range fighters were committed to support of the operations on the Continent, flying coastal patrols and reconnaissance operations, searching for German surface vessels. A rare engagement with enemy aircraft took place at 12.00 hours on 13 May when three Blenheim IVF's from No.254 Squadron, while on a patrol protecting the Royal Navy Destroyer HMS *Valentine* and a Dutch warship, in a position North East of Helder, conducting a bombardment of the East end of the Zuider Zee dam, were attacked by German aircraft, identified as four Me.110 fighters and a Junkers Ju.88 bomber. In the ensuing engagement one of the Blenheim' suffered light damage and one suffered "considerable damage", the British crews claiming a number of hits on the Me.110's.

The Blenheim IF Squadrons continued to fly daylight convoy patrols, local base patrols and fighter patrols off the coast of France towards the end of May and night patrols were flown to cover the evacuation of the BEF from Dunkirk in the last days of May and early June.

No.25 Squadron conducted two 'raid patrols' on the evening of 19 May; one aircraft taking off at 22.00 hours and the other at 22.45 hours. Another Blenheim took off on a 'raid patrol' at 00.30 hours in early morning of 20 May. A further two 'raid patrols were conducted at 00.35 hours in the early morning of 22 May, no enemy aircraft being encountered.

At 01.00 hours on the morning of 22 May a No.600 Squadron Blenheim was scrambled from Northolt to investigate a "bogey". Both the unidentified aircraft and the Blenheim flew over Northolt, the Blenheim tailing about 2 minutes behind. Having failed to intercept, the Blenheim landed back at Northolt.

On the 23rd, a No.600 Squadron Blenheim was flown to Hornchurch from where it flew to trips to Calais, France,escorted by Spitfires, to collect equipment being evacuated in the face of the German advance. On the 25th five No.600 Squadron Blenheim's flew convoy escort patrols from Biggin Hill, one aircraft being lost when it crashed on the return to base, the crew being killed.

On 24 May, No.25 Squadron was ordered to have six Blenheim's "brought to readiness to fly to Manston from where a sweep operation was to be conducted along the French and Belgian coasts. This operation was subsequently cancelled at 22.30 hours on 24 May.

While the BEF (British Expeditionary Force) was being evacuated from the continent, plans were afoot to re-equip No.25 Squadron with Westland Whirlwind single-seat, twin-engine high performance fighters, the first of which was handled by the Squadron at Bascombe Down on 30 May; no less than 4 No.25 Squadron pilots flying the Whirlwind the following day. Blenheim operations, however, continued spasmodically with a single raid patrol of three aircraft, coded ZK-G, ZK-K and ZK-F, taking off at 10.05 hours and landing at 10.45 on the night of 30 May.

On 1 June it seemed that No.25 Squadron would participate in the intense air operations over Dunkirk as the hard pressed BEF, and naval forces evacuating it, was being brought back to Britain. The squadron was ordered to readiness at 05.30 hours with orders to conduct a patrol from Dover to Dunkirk, but the operation was later cancelled.

Note: It was subsequently decided not to equip No.25 Squadron with the Whirlwind, this type going on to serve with 263 and 137 Squadrons; 25 Squadron eventually re-equipping with Bristol Beaufighters.

On the 20th of May No.604 Squadron was ordered to provide a Blenheim to transport the Chief of the Imperial Staff from France to Britain. On two occasions aircraft took off and awaited instructions, but were told to return to base.

604 Squadron flew no operations on the 21st, but early the following morning 'Green' Section of 'B' Flight, patrolling Dunkirk, encountered a Heinkel 111 some 12 miles to the North West of Dunkirk. The aircraft was attacked at about 0504 hours, 'Green' 1 (F/O Budd) and 'Green' 2 (P/O J.H.M. Rabone) firing bursts at the aircraft before it disappeared from view.

In the afternoon 'Red' Section of 'A' Flight, while conducting a patrol over Ramsgate, Kent, encountered 3 He.111 bombers approaching them from the South. Only Red 1 (S/Ldr. M.F. Anderson) was able to open fire, without result.

The No.604 Squadron Combat Reports for 22 May are reproduced below verbatim:

SECRET.   **COPY.**   **FORM "F".**

COMBAT REPORT.

(A)	
(B)	
(C)	**22/5/40.**
(D)	**Flight "A" Red Section. 604 Squadron.**
(E)	**THREE.**
(F)	**HEINKEL 111.**
(G)	**0504 hours.**
(H)	**Over Ramsgate.**
(J)	**9000 feet.**
(K)	**NIL.**
(L)	**NIL.**
(M)	**NIL.**
(N1)	**N/A.**
(N11)	**N/A.**
(P)	**See "R"**

GENERAL REPORT:-

Three a/c were ordered to take off at 0445 hours at a height of 10000 feet. I took off at 0452 hours and reached height at 0502 hours. I immediately saw three Heinkel 111's approaching from south in open VIC formation and as I was above I dived to attack and opened fire at 800 yards (Approx) range from astern. I closed in on the e/a and followed him through the tops of the clouds and got in 4 or 5 bursts at about 600 yards

range, but could not get e/a in sights for long due to clouds. We came to a clean patch and the e/a dived straight down to sea level. He was diving much faster than I, so I was unable to get in another burst. In spite of flying at plus 5 boost and an indicated speed of 225 m.p.h. I was unable to get any nearer. I then returned to Aerodrome and rendezvous with Red 2. I was told to escort a convoy from Dover to Boulogne and when 7 miles off Folkstone I was joined by Red 3. and Yellow Section. As we were nearing the French Coast at 0625 hours I noticed a line of A.A. fire coming towards me from N.E. I warned my a/c that E/A were about and then noticed that the A.A. bursts had descended to level of clouds. i.e. 7000 feet. As it was misty I sent Yellow Section down to patrol at 5,000 feet remaining at a good height myself. I warned "Foster" to warn them about the e/a in case they had not got my message due to bad R/T and at 0636 hours the leader of Yellow Section saw a Ju 88 which they tried to chase but were unable to get near enough to open fire. We continued patrolling and had to come down to 3000 feet when near Boulogne Harbour. As we approached Boulogne Harbour there was a large black cloud and a big fire burning on the water to the south of us. We escorted the convoy to practically the mouth of Boulogne Harbour when the middle ship of three Merchant-men appeared to run aground, it stopped and the other two circled round for some time. We stayed on patrol until 0815 hours. The weather had got worse and it was raining heavily, the clouds had come down to 100 feet and the visibility to 800 yards. I considered it unsafe to continue circling at this height with a formation so patrolled from outside the Harbour to Cape Gris Nez, but was gradually forced further away from the grounded ship. I therefore returned to base landing at 0853 hours.

Signed:- M.P. Anderson.

SECRET.   **COPY**.   **FORM "F"**.

COMBAT REPORT.

(A)	
(B)	
(C)	22/5/40.
(D)	Flight "B" Sqdn., 604.
(E)	ONE.
(F)	Heinkel 111.
(G)	Approx 1400 hrs.
(H)	12 miles N.W. of Dunkirk.
(J)	7000
(K)	NIL.
(L)	NIL.
(M)	NIL.
(N1)	N/A.
(N11)	N/A.
(P)	See "R"

GENERAL REPORT:-

I was patrolling with Green Section off the coast at Dunkirk at 8000 feet when my air gunner saw the Heinkel flying West about 3 miles North of us. I ordered the Section into line astern and closed to attack. The enemy twisted and dived into a cloud where he was lost, although Green 1 and Green 2 managed to get in good bursts before he disappeared. Rear gunfire was encountered from the E/A, but it appeared very ineffective. Three black objects, possibly bombs, were observed to fall from E/A after one of my bursts.

Signed:- G.O. Budd. F/O.
604 Squadron.

COPY.   FORM "F".

COMBAT REPORT.

(A)	
(B)	
(C)	22/5/40.
(D)	Flight "B" Sqdn., 604.
(E)	ONE.
(F)	Heinkel 111.
(G)	Approx 1400 hrs.
(H)	12 miles N.W. of Dunkirk.
(J)	7000 feet
(K)	NIL
(L)	NIL.
(M)	NIL.
(N1)	N/A.
(N11)	N/A.
(P)	See "R"

GENERAL REPORT:-

I was No.2 in Green Section off the coast at Dunkirk at 8000 feet and followed Green 1 in line astern to attack Heinkel. I fired one long burst at the enemy made a twisting dive, and later fired three short bursts at the retreating E/A., all probably out of range. I noticed a little tracer ammunition being fired from E/A rear gun, which was ineffective.

Signed:- Rabone P/O.
604 Squadron.

No.604 Squadron flew patrols over Dunkirk and Boulogne from dusk on the 23rd until dawn on the 24th. On the 23rd, 604 squadron provided an escort for three Motor Torpedo Boats sailing from Sheerness to Ostend, Belgium.

A single patrol was flown in the early hours of 25 May, the aircraft returning at 04.40 hours. On the 26th one of 604 Squadrons Blenheim's was damaged when a Gloster Gladiator, K8001, being used for formation landing practice, collided with Blenheim L6607; so unsuitable for the daylight fighter role was the Blenheim IF that 604 Squadron was equipping a Flight with obsolete Gladiator bi-plane fighters to conduct daytime local defence patrols. There were no operational patrols flown on the night of the 26th.

No.604 Squadron carried out night patrols over Dunkirk on the 27th to cover the BEF being evacuated back to Britain; one Blenheim, flown by F/O P.W.D. Heal, was hit by British anti-aircraft fire off North Foreland, suffering damage to the port wing formation light. It was subsequently determined that the culprit was a ship based machine-gun firing tracer. Blenheim's were also engaged by anti-aircraft fire "off shore at Dunkirk."

There were no patrols on the night of the 28th, but night patrols over Dunkirk were resumed on the night of the 29th; the last Blenheim on patrol landing at Tangmere due to bad weather at Manston. There were no noted operations by 604 Squadron Blenheim's on the night of the 29th, but during the day one Section flew an operational patrol over Manston at 10,000 ft. in Gloster Gladiator single-engine bi-plane fighters.

Night patrols over Dunkirk resumed on the night of 31 May, one Blenheim, L6680, being damaged when it "overshot the aerodrome boundary" when landing. On 2 June a patrol by Green Section encountered and chased an enemy aircraft "without success." Patrols were flown over Dunkirk on the night of 3 June; this being the last night of operations to cover the evacuation of the BEF. At the end of the patrols, two of the squadrons Blenheim's diverted to Biggin Hill and Detling respectively due to adverse weather.

There is much confusion among operational records in regards to a number of operations conducted by No.604 Squadron Blenheim's over Northern France. These operations were initially recorded as having taken place over the course of the nights of 17/18 and 18/19 June, but later altered to read that the operations had taken place over the course of the nights of 17/18 and 18/19 May. These alterations were applied to Fighter Command Intelligence Combat Reports and Pilot Combat Reports. Despite these alterations and the recording in the ORB's that the operations took place in May, available evidence would suggest that the operations actually took place in June as initially recorded in the Fighter Command Intelligence and Personal Combat Reports. For example, the aircraft were flying what could be termed early 'Intruder' operations over enemy held aerodromes, in this case Merville in Northern France; German aircraft would not have been operating from Merville on 17/19 May as it was still in Allied hands, not being captured by the Germans until the 27th. Another target area was St. Omar, which was not taken by the German 41st Corp until 23 May 1940. It would be logical to conclude, therefore, that the original dates of June on the Intelligence and Combat reports were in fact correct and that the later altered dates of May is in fact an error. The operations are detailed below.

Three 604 Squadron Blenheim's flew standing patrols over Bethune, Merville, St Pol and St Omer from Dusk on 17 June until dawn on the 18th. 'B' Flight flew night patrols over Bethune, Merville, St Pol and St Omer. During one patrol, flown by F/O A.S. Hunter, an aircraft was observed off Dunkirk with navigation lights on. This aircraft was attacked and claimed as shot down.

The Intelligence Patrol and Personal Combat Reports are here reproduced verbatim:

COPY. XIXH MAY?
18th. JUNE, 1940.

INTELLIGENCE PATROL REPORT.

On the evening of 17/6/40 (May? - handwritten) No.604 Squadron were ordered to put up a standing patrol over Bethune-Merville - St. Pol - St. Omer, from late dusk till dawn.
The following patrols were carried out:-
1st. patrol of 1 Blenheim left Manston at 2332 hrs. and landed Manston 0105 hrs.
2nd. : : 1 : : 0038 hrs. and landed Manston 0248 hrs.
3rd. : : 1 : : 0145 hrs. and landed Manston 0345 hrs.

The weather was good with a bright moon and no cloud or mist.
During all three patrols the black-out was absolutely perfect. No A.A. fire was encountered or seen anywhere.
On the first patrol however on a course St. Pol - St. Omer of 360° Mag. N. a few miles N.E. off St Omer, two white beacons were seen about 200 yards apart, in a large field with a hedge along one side.
The first beacon was revolving (like a lighthouse) and flashing a dash and the 2nd. Beacon (an uncovered light) immediately flashing 3 dots - thus flashing the morse letter "B", which occurred 12 times per minute. The pilot came down to 2000 ft. and fired at them, coming down to 500 feet. The lights were immediately switched off and our pilot climbed again and continued the journey home. These lights were again seen by the next two patrols however.
On the 2nd. Patrol nothing unusual happened, or was noticed by the pilot until coming home at 10,000 over Dunkirk he saw an A/C with navigations lights, and flying E.N.E. at about 100 feet and at about 160 m.p.h. He at once circled down and after travelling about 10 miles in E.N.E. direction came up behind and identified the plane as an HE.115 travelling about 200 yards off shore. This E/A/ was apparently quite unaware of the Blenheim and our pilot was able to get in a good burst of 5 seconds. The E/A then fired off a rocket which went up to an approx. height of 80 feet, and golden stars fell down in a stream like a "Golden Rain" firework completely blinding the pilot temporarily, for which purpose it appeared to be fired. He therefore circled round and found the E/A had descended from 100 feet to 4/6 feet above water level then he

fired off a further rocket similar to the first. No return fire from E/A was seen at all.

When this 2nd. rocket had faded, our pilot made another attack and closed in from 500 yards firing another burst of 5 seconds. The port engine of the He.115 caught fire and our A/C turned away due to windscreen being covered with oil similar to Glycol. It has been suggested that the E/A was running on heavy oil. As our A/C turned away the rear gunner had a final burst and saw the plane dive into the sea, extinguishing the fire in the port engine and the navigation lights went out. Our A/C then climbed and came home.

On the 3rd. patrol nothing further was seen or noticed.

THE BATTLE OF FRANCE— situation on 18 May 1940

Map showing the situation of the northern front on 18 May 1940. NZTEC

COMBAT REPORT

(A)

(B)   P.

(C)   18/6/40. (Handwritten - 18.5.40)

(D)   Flight "B"   Sqdn. 604. Green Section.

(E)   ONE.

(F)   HE. 115

(G)   0215 hours.

(H)   12 miles E.N.E. Dunkirk.

(J)   100 feet

(K)   ONE (conclusive)

(L)   NIL.

(M)   NIL.

(N1)   N/A.

(N11)   N/A.

(P)   See "R"

GENERAL REPORT:- (R)

By:- F/O. A.S. Hunter, flying as No.2 Green Section.

While returning from carrying out a standing patrol over Bethune - Merville - St. Pol - St. Omer I sighted from 10,000 feet A/C burning green light flying E.N.E. over Dunkirk at about 100 feet. I circled down and got behind A/C about 10 miles E.N.E. Dunkirk, at 100 feet, flying 160 m.p.h. 200 yards off-shore. I closed and regognised A/C as hostile and it was burning all navigation lights. I opened fire for about 5 seconds at 150 yards range, when a dazzling shower of gold stars was let off by E/A which completely obscured target from me. I turned and again got behind E/A about 500 yards, when another star-shell was fired. Immediately its brilliance had faded I closed again. E/A was now flying right down, only about 4/6 feet above sea. I gave another 5 Secs. burst and the port engine caught fire. Oil (resembling Glycol) then spread all over my A/C completely obscuring vision forward. As I turned the rear gunner fired a short burst and saw the E/A disappear into the sea, the lights and fire immediately being extinguished. I then returned to Baset the rounds fired from front guns were 200 from each, (ie. 1,000 in all).

Signed:-   A.S. HUNTER
                 Flying Officer

Night patrols were again flown over Dunkirk, Merville and St Omer on the 19th. During one of these patrols an enemy aircraft was observed with its navigation lights on, it subsequently being attacked by a Blenheim flown by F/O Skinner. As he attacked the aircraft the enemy lowered the undercarriage and shortly afterwards the aircraft was lost from view. Another Blenheim, flown by F/O G.O. Budd, on the same patrol as the above aircraft, encountered an enemy aircraft preparing to land on Merville aerodrome. The Blenheim attacked, a five second burst being fired, but the aircraft was lost to view shortly afterwards.

The Intelligence Patrol report for the above actions is reproduced below verbatim:

COPY. (Handwritten alteration to date) **May? See ORB in May**
                                   19th June 1940.   Manston.

INTELLIGENCE PATROL REPORT.

Two enemy aircraft, both thought to be HE. 111, which were flying low with their navigation lights on, were hit and damaged by pilots of 604 Sq. (Blenheims) on patrol duty over the Dunkirk – Merville - St. Omer areas on the night of 18 to 19/6/40. (This date is handwritten altered to May). **One enemy aircraft standing on Merville aerodrome was also damaged.**

Continuous patrols of one aircraft were carried out, the first aircraft taking off from Manston at 23.10 hrs. and the last landing at 0340 hrs.

The weather was good, visibility of about five miles. There was no cloud, but slight mist.

On the first patrol the pilot was about to return at 0025 hrs. 19/6, flying at 5,000 ft when he saw a Heinkel 111 flying N.E. at 4,000 ft about 15 miles S.E. of Dunkirk at about 160 m.p.h. The pilot,

F/O SKINNER.

stated that he was quite close when he saw the enemy aircraft which had the usual navigation lights burning. "I at once made a quarter attack," he stated, "and opened fire at about 350 yrds, using deflection, and saw my

tracer just ahead of engines. I closed to point blank range dead astern still firing and saw tracers enter the enemy aircraft right along the fuselage. The enemy aircraft used no evasive tactics, but flew straight and steady. No return fire was encountered. I used all my front gun ammunition (2,400 rounds) and then flew straight below and to the side, and my rear gunner put in a burst of 100 rounds at point blank range." The undercarriage of the enemy aircraft was seen to drop, and lights were extinguished before our pilot lost sight of it.

The second enemy aircraft was attacked at about 0100 hrs. over Merville aerodrome as it was about to land, with its navigation lights on, from a height of about 3,000 feet. The Blenheim pilot,

F/O. BUDD.

stated:- "I immediately made a stern attack from about 100 yards, closing to about 50 yards, and gave a burst of about 5 secs. I saw tracer enter the enemy aircraft. Return fire came from the top turret but soon ceased. The proportion of tracers used by the enemy aircraft appeared to be higher than in our guns." The return fire was not accurate. Our pilot, whose windscreen became covered with oil, lost sight of the enemy aircraft when it switched off its lights. He saw another enemy aircraft standing on the aerodrome with its lights on. "I dived from 1,500 feet to 500 ft," he stated, "and put in a burst of about 80 rounds per gun at the A/c into which I saw the tracers enter. During this attack my rear gunner saw flashes of yellow, green and red, and I saw machine gun tracer bullets directed at me, but we were not hit."

After climbing, and then diving to 1,500 ft., the pilot saw seven to ten aircraft landing and taking off. He received a machine gun bullet in the self-sealing petrol tank. No damage was done.

The pilot saw the flare path on MERVILLE aerodrome, but no flood lights. No obstruction lights were placed on hangers or buildings. The flare path was in a straight line, with several lights close together at one end, but no "T" was observed. The lights were not shielded from above and could easily be seen 5,000 feet. The enemy aircraft appeared to be using their own headlights when landing. An enemy aircraft which was machine gunned from the ground and let off three Red flares together and a white flare a second or two later, causing the attack to cease.

In view of reports of red flares, it is worthwhile considering whether the enemy aircraft signals consist of three flares which are constant, and another coloured flare which changes from time to time. It would be instructive, too, if some information could be obtained on the night flying, landing, and taking-off procedure of the German air force. This would enable pilots to take advantage of such procedures when attacking aircraft on aerodromes which are being used for night flying.

All pilots state that the black-out over France was very good and that they encountered no searchlights or a/c fire. The two great fires from petrol tanks at Dunkirk were still burning. A beacon flashed a continuous white light about eight miles on a bearing of 60 degrees Mag. From Merville. This bearing should prove of great assistance to other aircraft carrying out the same patrol. Three white beacons were flashing approximately 25 miles East of Dunkirk, and two red flashing beacons were seen near Merville. CALMS lighthouse was flashing.

No fighter enemy aircraft appears to be used for night defensive. All out pilots and aircraft returned serviceable.

It was suggested by F/O Budd that the carrying of small bombs by Blenheim aircraft on this type of operation might prove useful, for when aerodromes are being used by aircraft landing and taking off with navigation lights on, our aircraft could dive down and drop bombs on the flare path, thereby causing confusion and damage to aircraft landing and taking-off, if the timing of the bombing was correctly judged.

Whilst it appears quite easy to make interception of enemy aircraft burning navigation lights, it would appear to be impossible to see the aircraft once navigation lights are extinguished, even on a clear night.

COMBAT REPORT.

(A)	
(B)	
(C)	19/6/40. (Handwritten alteration to May)
(D)	"A" Flight 604 Sqdn. Yellow Sect. No.2.
(E)	ONE.
(F)	H.E. 111.
(G)	0025 hrs.
(H)	15 miles S.E. of Dunkirk.
(J)	4000 feet
(K)	ONE DAMAGED
(L)	NIL.
(M)	NIL.
(N1)	N/A.
(N11)	N/A.
(P)	See "R"

GENERAL REPORT:- (R)

I took off from Manston at 2110 hours 18/6/40 to carry out patrol Dunkirk-Merville-Bethume-St. Omer and St. Pol. I had finished my patrol and was returning to base when at 0025 hours 19/6/40 and at a height of approx. 5000 feet I saw a HE.111 flying N.E. about 15 miles S.E. of Dunkirk at 4000 feet and flying at approx. 160 mph. I was quite close to the E/A when I saw it flying with usual Red, Green, and White navigation lights burning and I at once made a quarter attack and opened fire at about 350 yards, using deflection and saw my tracer just ahead of engines. I closed to point blank range dead astern still firing and saw tracers enter the E/A right along fuselage. The E/A used no evasive tactics but flew straight and steady. No return fire was encountered. I used all my front gun ammunition and then flew straight below and to the side and my rear gunner put in a burst of 100 rounds at point blank range. The undercarriage was seen to drop and navigation lights were extinguished. I then lost sight of the E/A. I then flew home to base. No searchlights were seen during the whole patrol and no A.A. fire was encountered. 2400 rounds were fired by front guns and 100 rounds from rear gun.

SECRET.   COPY.   FORM "F".

COMBAT REPORT.

(A)
(B)
(C)   19/6/40. (Handwritten alteration to May)
(D)   "A" Flight No.604 Sqdn. Sect. Yellow. No.2
(E)   TWO.
(F)   H.E. 111. (presumed)
(G)
(H)   OVER MERVILLE AERODROME.
(J)   Approx. 3000 feet
(K)   TWO DAMAGED
(L)   NIL.
(M)   NIL.
(N1)   N/A.
(N11)   N/A.
(P)   See "R"

GENERAL REPORT:-   (R)

By:-   F/O Budd.

I took off from Manston at 0011 hours 19/6/40 to carry out patrol
Dunkirk-Merville-St. Omer area. At about 0100 hours and whilst over
Merville Aerodrome and at approx. 3000 feet I saw an E/A which I took
to be a HE.111. about to land, burning usual Red, Green and White
navigation lights. I immediately made a stern attack from about 100 yards
closing to about 50 yards and gave a burst of about 5 secs. I saw tracer
enter the E/A. Return fire came from top turret and soon ceased. The
proportion of tracers used by the E/A appeared to be higher than in our
own guns. The return fire was inaccurate. My windscreen became
covered with oil and as the E/A had apparently switched off his
navigation lights I was unable to see it again. I then circled the
aerodrome and saw another E/A stationary on ground and lights
burning. I dived from 1500 feet to 500 feet and put in a burst of about 80
rounds per gun into the A/C into which I saw the tracers enter. During
this attack my rear gunner saw flashes of Yellow, Green and Red and I
saw machine gun tracer bullets directed at me, but we were not hit. I then
climbed to about 8000 feet and then came down to 1500 feet and circled
again and saw about 7 to 10 A/C landing and taking off. I again received

machine gun fire and the A/C was hit but not seriously. One bullet went into the petrol tank, but this being self sealing the bullet did no damage. I then returned to base. No A.A. or searchlights were seen during the whole patrol. 1150 rounds were fired by front guns. On Merville Aerodrome I saw the flare path, but no flood light nor were obstruction lights placed on hangers or buildings. The flare path was in a straight line with several lights close together at one end. The lights were not shielded from above and could easily be seen at 5000 feet. The E/A appeared to use their own headlights when landing. I observed one E/A being attacked by machine gun fire from the ground and this machine promptly let off three Red flares together and a second or so afterwards a white flare and the ground attack ceased. About 8 miles on a bearing of 60 degrees Mag. Merville I saw a beacon flashing a continuous White light.

During the latter half of May and early June, apart from the Blenheim IF squadrons that flew night patrols over the Dunkirk during the evacuation of the BEF and other allied forces, and other squadrons flying convoy escort patrols, the general trend for the Fighter Command Blenheim IF Squadrons was gearing towards their primary role of providing a small measure of night defense against enemy aircraft operating over Britain.

No.23 Squadron Night Interception Patrols, June 1940

Throughout May No.23 Squadron flew no operational sorties other than co-operation flights with other commands. On 4 June, No.23 Squadron conduced six night patrols over the East Coast Sector; no enemy aircraft being encountered. Nine Blenheim's flew night interception patrols the following night; again no enemy aircraft being encountered, although crews reported "bomb flashes observed on ground." On the night of 6 June, seven Blenheim's flew interception patrols; no enemy aircraft being encountered. Records are patchy, but it appears that eight Blenheim's flew patrols on the night of 7 June and five on the night of 8 June. There were no patrols on 9 or 10 June, but two aircraft flew night patrols on 11 June; four patrols were flown on 12 June, 4 on 13 June, 4 on 15 June; 2 on 16 June, and 4 on 17 June, all without encountering any enemy aircraft.

The uneventful patrols of the previous weeks was contrasted by a sudden burst of drama for the squadron on the night of 18 June. Seven Blenheim's were flown on night interception patrols, one of which, crewed by F/Lt Duke-Woolley (pilot) and AC Bell (air gunner) engaged an enemy aircraft, identified as a He.111, claiming it shot down near Sheringham, Norfolk. The Blenheim was apparently damaged, returning to base on one engine. Another Blenheim, flown by S/Ldr O'Brien, engaged an aircraft identified as a He.111, claiming it shot down near Newmarket. As the Blenheim broke off from the attack it apparently "developed an uncontrollable spin." S/Ldr. O'Brien successfully abandoned the aircraft and descended by parachute. P/O King-Clark apparently bailed out but was killed when he struck the Blenheim's starboard airscrew. The air gunner, Cpl. Little, failed to exit the stricken aircraft and was killed when it crashed.

Prior to the loss of S/Ldr. O'Brien's aircraft, another Blenheim, flown by Sgt. Close, was shot down while engaging an enemy aircraft; the pilot was killed, but the air gunner, LAC Karasek, bailed out and landed by parachute.

The No.23 Squadron Intelligence Combat Report and Personal Combat Reports for the night of 18/19 June are reproduced below verbatim:

SECRET.   **FORM 'F'.**

INTELLIGENCE COMBAT REPORT.

(A) **K1**

(B)

(C) **18/19-6-40**

(D) **Flights 'A' and 'B', Squadron 23.**

(E) **About 7 but many more known to be about.**

(F) **Heinkel 111's.**

(G) **22.30 – 03.50 hours.**

(H) **N.E. Kings Lynn and 10 miles E. Newmarket.**

(J) **8,000 ft. – 16,000 ft.**

(K) **2 confirmed**

(L) **2.**

(M) **2.**

(N1) **Searchlights assisted in picking out E/A.**

(N2) **No.**

(P) **Bursts of fire ranging from 250-20 yards.**

(R) **GENERAL REPORT.**

On night of 18/19 June Squadron 23 were ordered on Search-light Co-operation but owing to considerable E/A activity they were then ordered to intercept.

First information of interception came from Sgt. Close who was unable to gain on E/A. Shortly after he announced he was gaining on him and finally could see the Nazi crosses and swastikas. It was later reported that E/A had shot him down close to Sutton Bridge. The A.G. L.A.C. Angus who "baled out" has since reported that Sgt. Close approached E/A from astern and slightly underneath but did not fire or carry out any evasive tactics. E/A lower rear gunner gave full burst to starboard engine, second and third bursts entered cockpit, killing pilot who was then endeavouring to "bale out". The machine crashed in flames, confirmed by S/Ldr. O'Brien and F/Lt. Duke Wooley.

F/Lt. Duke Woolley at 8,000 feet near Kings Lynn saw E/A shoot down Sgt. Close (whose body has since been picked up). He proceeded to chase E/A and after a short while he caught up with him and after two bursts of 5 or 6 seconds his A.G. reported port engine on fire and tail plane aglow. Both seemed certain that this machine, an He.111, would not reach home. When F/Lt., Duke Woolley delivered his attack he found that he was only doing 130 m.p.h. and the E/A about 110 m.p.h. so that he overshot him and to avoid hitting him turned steeply away receiving fire from the rear gunner. He returned to base with starboard engine U/S. This E/A casualty was shortly after confirmed by its crashing at Clay-on-Sea (Nr. Sheringham). Four prisoners were taken, one being Major von Coeler, who volunteered information to the Military that he was the leader of a formation of 15 A/C which had been broken up much earlier by A.A. fire. He also said that he had shot down one of our fighters, presumably Sgt. Close, and had then been shot down by another of our fighters, presumably F/Lt. Duke Woolley.

S/Ldr. O'Brien tackled an E/A picked out and held by searchlights and from his information shot it down in vicinity of Newmarket. This is confirmed by the fact E/A crashed 5 miles E. of Cambridge. 1 crew killed, 1 officer and 2 Sergeants captured and taken to Duxford. His machine then got out of control in a vertical dive and gave orders to abandon the aircraft. His A.G. failed to free himself and his passenger. P/O King Clark was killed in "bailing out". Squadron Leader O'Brien then broke free and got away safely by parachute and his machine crashed and was burnt out – He thought that he had been hit by AC/AC but this is not confirmed. F/Lt. Knight and P/O Pattison both saw E/A but were unable to get near them. It would appear that on interceptions made, E/A throttled back to await our A/C to overshoot them.

From inspection of E/A brought down on Clay-on-Sea (He.111's) they have 4 guns one firing from top of fuselage aft and one underneath fuselage, also firing aft. Besides these guns, there were two other blister guns, firing sideways, but there was no forward armament.

According to the inspection of this E/A there was no cannon armament.

Regarding camouflage of E/A Squadron Leader O'Brien stated that the under surface of the wings of the E/A were a very pale blue appearing almost white in the moonlight.

8 Blenheims carried out individual patrols during the night. 5 interceptions were made in which:-
1   2 He.111's were confirmed shot down.
2   2 Blenheims were shot down with 3 personnel killed.
3   Of the five interceptions combats occurred in three cases; in the other two the E/A made use of their superior speed and the Blenheims were unable to overhaul them.

SECRET.   FORM "F".

COMBAT REPORT.

(A) K1
(B)
(C) 18/19/6/40
(D) Flight B.   Squadron 23.
(E) One.
(F) Heinkel 111. MK.V.
(G) 1250.
(H) 6 Ms.   N.E. Kings Lynn.
(J) 8,000 ft.
(K) 1 probable.
(L) Nil.
(M) Nil.
(N1) Yes.
(N2) No.
(P) 50+150 yards.
    5-6 seconds.

(R) **GENERAL REPORT.**

Whilst flying at 6,000 feet 3m. N.E. Kings Lynn observed aircraft subsequently identified as He.111 Mk.v. held in search-lights at 8,000 feet. Time 12.45. Observed ball of fire which I took to be fighter Blenheim in flames break away from behind tail of E/A. Climbed to engage E/A and attacked from below tail after searchlights were no longer holding. Range 50 yards. E/A returned fire and appeared to throttle back suddenly. Own speed 130-140 m.p.h. Estimate E/A slowed to 110 m.p.h. Delivered five attacks. Air gunner fired seven short bursts at varying ranges. After last front gun attack Air gunner reported port engine E/A on fire. Returned base and landed: starboard engine U/S. Several bullet holes in wings and fuselage of own aircraft including hit in starboard wing and rear fuselage by cannon.

Signature   Duke Woolley. F/Lt.,
  Section Blue.
   Flight B.
Squadron 23.

Form "F".

COMBAT REPORT.

(A) K1
(B)
(C) 18/19-6-40.
(D) Flight "A".   Squadron 23.
(E) ONE.
(F) Heinkel 111. mk.V.
(G) 1.25.
(H) About ten miles from Newmarket.
(J)   12,000 ft.
(K) ONE
(L) ONE.
(M) TWO.
(N1) Held E/A nearly whole time.
(N2) No.
(P) 100 yds. Several bursts.

.

(R)   Intercepted 1 He.111K 12,000 feet in vicinity of Newmarket. Opened fire at E/A with rear gun from position below and in front (E/A held by searchlight). E/A turned port and dived, I then gave him several long bursts with front guns from 50-100 yards range, and saw clouds of smoke from starboard engine, also lesser amount of smoke from port engine. I then overshot E/A and passed very close below and in front of him. My rear gunner put a burst at close range into cockpit. E/A disappeared in diving turn apparently out of control. Suddenly lost control of my aircraft which spun violently to left. Failing to recover from spin I ordered crew to abandon aircraft and followed navigator out through top hatch. E/A crashed about 10 miles from Newmarket.

Previous to my combat I saw aircraft fall in flames in vicinity of Kings Lynn. Subsequently found that this was Sergeant Close.

(Signature) J.O'Brien, S/Ldr.,
Flight   "A".
Squadron 23.
Aircraft left ground 0030 hours.
Aircraft crashed 0125 hours.

On the night of 18/19 June, No.29 Squadron claimed three German bombers destroyed for the loss of a Blenheim.

On the night of 19 June, four No.23 Squadron Blenheim's were flown on night interception patrols. At least one enemy aircraft was observed, but no interception took place. There were no operational patrols on the night of 20 June, but three Blenheim's were flown on night interception patrols on the 21st; three flown on the 22nd, four on the 24th, seven on the 25th, six on the 26th and five on the 27th, all without encountering enemy aircraft.

On the 28th, two night interception patrols were flown; one Blenheim, P/O Williams/P/O Atkinson, engaged a Heinkel 111 which was intercepted "in the vicinity of Norwich" at an altitude of 16,000 ft. The Blenheim opened fire at a range of 300 yards down to 50 yards; 600 rounds being fired. The aircraft was claimed damaged and probably not able to reach base.

The Intelligence and Combat Reports for the interception on the night of 28/29 June is reproduced below verbatim:

INTELLIGENCE REPORT.

SECRET.   **FORM "F".**

(A) **K1.**
(B) **Red Patrol Line.**
(C) **28/29-6-40.**
(D) **A.   23.**
(E) **1.**
(F) **He.111.**
(G) **0042 Hrs.**
(H) **Approx. S.E. of Norwich.**
(J) **16,000 ft.**
(K) **1 probable.**
(L) **Nil.**
(M) **Nil.**
(N1) **Yes.**
(N2) **Nil.**
(P) **Bursts of fire ranging from 350-100 yards.**
(R) **GENERAL REPORT.**

On night 28/29 June two aircraft of 23 sqdn. were ordered on patrol – red 4 and red 7.

Near Norwich Red 7 noticed S/Lt. intersection which he proceeded to investigate and which led him in a southerly direction at about 16000 ft. at 0030 hours. At about 0035 one S/Lt. picked out E/A and this was quickly followed by about 12 other lights and all held E/A in a small circle of light and at 0039 Red 7 who had then distinguished E/A as an He.111 was seen by S/Lt. to open his attack. The fire was opened by the air gunner from underneath with the enemy going in opposite direction. Red 7 then turned quickly around on to E/A tail and opened fire from dead astern. And slightly above at 350 yards closing to 100 yards. The A/G could see the first few rounds passing over the E/A so Red 7 dipped his nose and fired a burst of about 7 seconds – he then noticed tracer bullets being fired by E/A's two rear guns so opened fire again with a further burst of about 3 seconds using in all 450 rounds per gun. All fire then ceased from enemy rear guns Red 7 then passed below and in front giving his A/G opportunity of firing one full pan of 100 rounds at point blank range. He fitted another pan but trigger mechanism failed. Red 7 then broke away and was preparing to make a further frontal attack when S/Lts. doused and he did not see the E/A again. Both pilot and A/G although not seeing the E/A crash were of the opinion it would never reach its base. Red 7 states he saw bombs falling, this being confirmed by S/Lts. Who state that bombs dropped at M9295 at 0040 hours. Observer post F3 report having seen Fighter chasing E/A at Approx M7979 and that one engine of latter A/C was put out of action but they did not see it crash. During engagement E/A reduced his speed considerably thereby forcing our fighter to throttle his engines right back but even then overshooting E/A. Both pilot and A/G of Red 7 report very inaccurate shooting of E/A as our fighter was not hit once. Red 7 P/O Williams and A/G P/O. Atkinson took off at 2225 hrs. and landed 0133 hours. The pilot fired about 450 rounds per front gun. The A/G used about 2 - ½ pans of 100 rounds each.

(Signed)   E. MITCHELL, P/O.,
Squadron Intelligence Officer,
No.23, Squadron.

SECRET.   FORM "F".

Certified True Copy.

(sgnd) E. Mitchell P/O.
Intelligence Officer,
No.23 Squadron.

COMBAT REPORT.

(A) K.1.
(B) Ordered to Patrol Red Patrol Line at 12,000 at 2225 hours.
(C) 28/29/6/40.
(D) Flight A.   Squadron 23.
(E) 1 He.111.
(F) He.111.
(G) 0042.
(H) Approx. S.E. of Norwich.
(J) 16,000 ft.
(K) 1 probable.
(L) Nil.
(M) Nil.
(N1) Excellent.
(N2) Nil.
(P) 300 feet 2 seconds.
(R) GENERAL REPORT.

I was ordered on red patrol at 12,000 feet and left the ground at 2225 hours. I was carrying out my patrol near Norwich when I sighted a good intersection of searchlight at about 16,000 feet moving approximately south. I followed this intersection of lights at full throttle when a large number of incendiary bombs were dropped immediately below me. Soon after this the intersection changed direction to the right and I followed then for approximately three minutes when the intersection appeared to reverse direction. I then turned through 180° and continued to follow the S/L's for about three minutes when A/C was illuminated by one S/L, the other lights swung on to the target and I identified E/A as an He.111. He did a steep turn and flew past us on the starboard side and slightly above. My A/G fired a short burst at about 100 yards. I turned quickly round on to the Heinkel's tail and opened fire from dead astern and slightly above at 350 yards. This burst of about 7 seconds indicated incendiary bullets striking E/A fuselage. When I finished my burst I saw tracer bullets fired at me from the E/A two rear guns and I opened fire again with a 3 second burst; all fire from the E/A rear guns then ceased and we passed underneath and my rear gunner opened fire just below and in front at point blank range. The E/A took evasive action by turning off and I resumed my attack from below and in front. My rear gunner fired a short burst and he ran out of ammunition on the pan. I broke away to the right intending to renew a front gun attack but the lights doused and I could not find E/A again. I was then ordered to return to base.

Took off – 2225 hours.
Landed – 0135 hours.

Signature D.A. Williams P/O.
A Flight.
Squadron 23.

The following night three interception patrols were flown; three more being flown on the 30th, all without encountering enemy aircraft.

No.25 Squadron Night Interception Patrols, June 1940

One Blenheim, code I (P/O Rofe/AC McCormack), took-off from North Weald on a defensive 'X' Raid patrol at 22.55 hours on 7 June. No interception was made, but the Blenheim was fired at by British ground defence machine guns, but sustained no damage, landing at 23.25 hours.

A single Blenheim was flown on an X Raid patrol on the 9th and four patrols, totaling 5.30 hours flying time, were flown on the night of the 18/19th, one Blenheim being fired at by British anti-aircraft fire.
Note: The patrol on the 9th is not listed in the Squadron ORB Form 541, but is detailed in the Form 540. Only one sortie is listed in the Form 541 for the 19th and none for the 18th, but all four are detailed in the Form 540

No.25 Squadron moved from North Weald to Martlesham Heath on the 19th, following which no patrols were flown until the 21st, when a single 'X' Raid patrol was flown, Blenheim 'H' taking off at 01.05 hours and landing at 01.50 hours.
Note: This sortie is listed in the Form 541, but is absent from the Form 540.

A single 'X' Raid patrol was flown on the 25th and a Raid patrol of three Blenheim's was apparently flown on the 26th; the aircraft taking off at 04.20 hours.
Note: The sorties for the 25th and 26th are not listed in the Form 541, but are detailed in the Form 540.

A single patrol was flown on the 27th, Blenheim 'H' taking off at 23.15 hours, landing at 00.45 on the 28th. Blenheim 'B' took-off on patrol at 00.50 hours on the 28th, landing at 10.10 hours. Blenheim 'H' took-off on patrol at 23.50 hours on the 28th, landing at 01.25 hours on the 29th.

Note: The sorties for the 27th, 28th and 29th are listed in the Form 541, but are absent from the Form 540.

As well as the operational sorties, the Blenheim Squadrons flew many non-operational co-operation sorties with other commands and conducted training flights, particularly with AI (Airborne Interception) equipment and RDF (Radio Direction Finding) trials.

5

POSTCRIPT

Following the losses of 10 May the writing was on the wall for the Blenheim IF as a day fighter. Fighter Commands Blenheim IF's squadrons continued to fly convoy escort and local airfield defense patrols during daylight hours, with the occasional fighter sweep, but to all intents and purposes the Blenheim's career as a long-range day fighter was over in the European theatre where strong enemy fighter opposition could be expected.

As June rolled into July 1940 the Blenheim IF Squadrons turned increasingly to the night fighter role, forming the backbone of Britain's small night fighter force as the war moved into the phase known as the Battle of Britain; the type being progressively replaced by the more capable Bristol Beaufighter and Boston Havoc during the winter months of 1940/41.

The Blenheim IF was also deployed to other theatres, including the Middle East, where the type served during the first few years of the war until replaced by more modern equipment.

.

Top: Crew member climbs into a No.29 Squadron Blenheim MK.IF preparing for a night patrol from Colby Grange, Lincolnshire, in October 1940. Above: Blenheim MK.IF's equipped squadrons in other theatres. This No.211 Squadron aircraft, L6670, UQ-R, is landing at Menidi-Tatoi, Greece, following a raid on Italian forces in Albania in 1941. RAF

APPENDICES

Blenheim MK.IF Squadrons September 1939 - June 1940

No.23 - Winter 1938
No.25 - 10 December 1938
No.29 - December 1938
No.64 - Late 1938 - April 1940
No.92 - 10 October 1939 - March 1940
No.145 - 10 October 1939 - March 1940
No.219 - 4 October 1939
No.222 - 5 October 1939 - March 1940
No.229 - 6 October 1939 - March 1940
No.233 - October 1939 - February 1940. One Flight only equipped with Blenheim's
No.234 - October 1939 - March 1940. Squadron operated a mix of Battle's, Gauntlet and Blenheim's
No.235 – October 1939 (Formed on 30 October 1939, receiving Blenheim's in December). Coastal Command
No.236 - 31 October 1939
No.242 - December 1939 - January 1940
No.245 - October 1939 - March 1940
No.248 - 30 October 1939 (received Blenheim's in December 1939). Transferred to Coastal Command February 1940
No.254 - 30 October 1939. Transferred to Coastal Command in April 1940 and re-equipped with Blenheim IVF's
No.600 - January 1939
No.601 - January 1939 - March 1940
No.604 - 1939

The dates given are for the respective squadron formations or re-equipment with Blenheim's. The dates for replacement of Blenheim's with other aircraft types is given when that re-equipment took place prior to June 1940.

APPENDIX II

Specification

Bristol Blenheim MK.IF

Power plant: 2 x Bristol Mercury VIII nine-cylinder air-cooled piston engines, each rated at 840 hp.
Span: 56 ft. 4.in (17.14 m)
Wing area: 469 sq. ft.
Length: 39 ft. 9-in (12.11 m)
Height: 12 ft. 10 in
Weight: 8,100lb empty and 12,250 lb. loaded
Speed: 295 mph (460 km/h) at 15,000 ft. (4572 m)
Ceiling: 32,000 ft.
Range: 1,125 miles
Armament: 4 x 0.303 in Browning machine guns in a ventral fairing and a single 0.303 Vickers K machine gun mounted in a semi-retractable hydraulically operated dorsal turret.
Crew: 2; pilot and air gunner, but could accommodate 3 when observer carried.

Note: The maximum speed quoted above would have been achieved during trials, but was unrealistic under normal operating conditions. In reality the Blenheim IF often had difficulty in achieving enough speed to intercept enemy bombers like the He.111, which had quoted lower maximum speed. Than the Blenheim.

GLOSSARY

A/C	Aircraft
AC	Aircraft's Man
AI	Airborne Interception
DH	de Havilland
E/A	Enemy Aircraft
F/Lt.	Flight Lieutenant
Flying Officer	Flying Officer
F/Sgt.	Flight Sergeant
GR	General purpose Reconnaissance
He.	Heinkel
HMS	His Majesty's Ship
Ju	Junkers
LAC	Leading Aircraft's Man
Me.	Messerschmitt
No.	Number
OTU	Operational Training Unit
P/O	Pilot Officer
RAF	Royal Air Force
RAuxAF	Royal Auxiliary Air Force
RDF	Radio Direction Finder
R/T	Radio Transmitter
Sgt.	Sergeant
S/L	Searchlight
S/Ldr.	Squadron Leader
S/Lts	Searchlights

BIBLIOGRAPHY

CAB 106 Account of Military and Naval Operations in The Netherlands from 10th - 14th May 1940

No.23 Squadron Operations Record Book Form 540 September 1939 - June 1940

No.23 Squadron Operations Record Book Form 541 September 1939 - June 1940

No.25 Squadron Operations Record Book Form 540 September 1939 - June 1940

No.25 Squadron Operations Record Book Form 541 September 1939 - June 1940

No.25 Squadron Narrative of the raid on the seaplane base at Borkum, November 1939

No.600 Squadron Operations Record Book Form 540/541 for May/June 1940

No.600 Squadron Narrative of the attack on Rotterdam aerodrome

No.600 Squadron narrative of patrols in the afternoon of 10 May 1940

No.601 Squadron Operations Record Book Form 540 1939/40

No.601 Squadron Narrative of the raid on the seaplane base at Borkum, November 1939

No.604 Squadron Operations Record Book Form 540 Jan-June 1940

No.604 Squadron Operations Record Book Form 541 May/June 1940

Fighter Command Form 'F' Report on Raid on Beaches at The Hague, 10 May 1940

History of the Second World War, The RAF 1939-45 Volume I, 1953 HMSO

History of the Second World War, The Defence of the United Kingdom, 1957 HMSO

History of the Second World War, The War in France and Flanders 1939-1940, 1954 HMSO

The German Air Force in France and the Low Countries 1940, Volume I-III

Combat Report, No.604 Squadron 29 January 1940

Combat Report - Blenheim's "Q", "N", "R", No.254 Squadron - 22 February, 1940

Coastal Command Combat Report, No.22/40. No.254 Squadron 13 May 1940

Intelligence Patrol Report, No.604 Squadron 18 June/May? 1940

Intelligence Patrol Report, No.604 Squadron 19 June/May? 1940

Intelligence Combat Report, 23 Squadron, 18/19 June 1940

Combat Reports, 23 Squadron, 18/19 June 1940

Intelligence Report, 23 Squadron, 28/29 June 1940

Combat Reports, 23 Squadron, 28/29 June 1940

In addition hundreds of miscellaneous pages of documents; development, operational, command and political were consulted.

ABOUT THE AUTHOR

Hugh, a historian and author, has published in excess of thirty books; non-fiction and fiction, writing under his own name as well as utilising two different pseudonyms. He has also written for several international magazines, whilst his work has been used as reference for many other projects ranging from the aviation industry, international news corporations, film media to encyclopedias and the computer gaming industry. He currently resides in his native Scotland

Other titles by the Author include

Hurricane IIB Combat Log - 151 Wing RAF, North Russia 1941
RAF Meteor Jet Fighters in World War II, an Operational Log
Typhoon IA/B Combat Log - Operation Jubilee, August 1942
Defiant MK.I Combat Log - Fighter Command, May-September 1940
Eurofighter Typhoon - Storm over Europe
Tornado F.2/F.3 Air Defence Variant
British Battlecruisers of World War 1 - Operational Log, July 1914-June 1915
Boeing X-36 Tailless Agility Flight Research Aircraft
X-32 - The Boeing Joint Strike Fighter
X-35 - Progenitor to the F-35 Lightning II
X-45 Uninhabited Combat Air Vehicle
North American F-108 Rapier
F-84 Thunderjet - Republic Thunder
USAF Jet Powered Fighters - XP-59-XF-85
XF-92 - Convairs Arrow
The Battle Cruiser Fleet at Jutland
Light Battlecruisers and the 2nd Battle of Heligoland Bight
Saab Gripen, The Nordic Myth
American Teens
Dassault Rafale, The Gallic Squall
Boeing F/A-18E/F Super Hornet